The S
Informat.

ALSO BY ROBERT HAUPTMAN

*Documentation: A History and Critique of Attribution,
Commentary, Glosses, Marginalia, Notes, Bibliographies,
Works-Cited Lists, and Citation Indexing and Analysis*
(McFarland, 2008)

Ethics and Librarianship
(McFarland, 2002)

Journal of Information Ethics, editor
(McFarland, 1991–present)

The Scope of Information Ethics

Challenges in Education, Technology, Communications, Medicine and Other Domains

ROBERT HAUPTMAN

Foreword by JOHANNES K. BRITZ
Afterword by ELIZABETH A. BUCHANAN

McFarland & Company, Inc., Publishers
Jefferson, North Carolina

I thank Kellie of the Mark Skinner Library in Manchester, Vermont, for acquiring the many books that I requested.

LIBRARY OF CONGRESS CATALOGUING-IN-PUBLICATION DATA

Names: Hauptman, Robert, 1941– author.
Title: The scope of information ethics : challenges in education, technology, communications, medicine and other domains / Robert Hauptman.
Description: Jefferson, North Carolina : McFarland & Company, Inc., Publishers, 2019. | Includes bibliographical references and index.
Identifiers: LCCN 2019000182 | ISBN 9781476675671 (softcover : acid free paper) ∞
Subjects: LCSH: Information technology—Moral and ethical aspects. | Information science—Moral and ethical aspects.
Classification: LCC QA76.9.M65 H38 2019 | DDC 175—dc23
LC record available at https://lccn.loc.gov/2019000182

BRITISH LIBRARY CATALOGUING DATA ARE AVAILABLE

ISBN (print) 978-1-4766-7567-1
ISBN (ebook) 978-1-4766-3530-9

Front cover image © 2019 ivanastar/iStock

Printed in the United States of America

McFarland & Company, Inc., Publishers
Box 611, Jefferson, North Carolina 28640
www.mcfarlandpub.com

"It is the sheer breadth and inclusiveness of information ethics that makes it an exciting area."—Paul Sturges

Table of Contents

Table of Contents

Foreword
by Johannes K. Britz

As a lifelong mountaineer, Bob Hauptman has pursued many vistas. In this far-ranging monograph, he puts forward a similarly expansive view of the field of information ethics. His analysis of the ethical challenges across various sectors of our world addresses both fundamental ethical principles as they relate to information and the ways in which we collectively avoid full engagement with and accountability for our actions within the academy and beyond.

Every chapter sparks thoughtful reflection and a desire to further investigate the compelling ideas he puts forward: How is it possible that misinformation has spread so widely? To what extent does peer review foster mediocrity and mendacity? How is that so many, from across the political spectrum, have come to embrace restrictions on the free flow of information? What do the concepts of "the integrity of the person" and "privacy" mean in the advent of new technologies with the potential to objectify us? These are questions that we must grapple with—not in an abstract way, but in recognition of what is at stake on a practical basis for our democratic institutions and in the sense-making activities we engage in as human beings.

Denis Diderot, coauthor of the great *Encylopédie*, thought of the "vast realm of the sciences as an immense landscape scattered with patches of dark and light. The goal towards which we must work is either to extend the boundaries of the patches of light, or to increase their number." This book, in offering a truly encyclopedic overview of the crucial-to-our-times field of information ethics, extends the boundaries of light.

Foreword by Johannes K. Britz

In writing it, Hauptman has drawn on a lifetime of scholarship that gives weight to his identification of the challenges we face in the "knowledge society."

Johannes K. Britz is the provost, vice chancellor for academic affairs and professor in the School of Information Studies at the University of Wisconsin–Milwaukee (britz@uwm.edu)

Abbreviations

AI   Artificial Intelligence
AIA   American Institute of Architects
AMA   American Medical Association
CAT   Computerized Axial Tomography
CDA   Communications Decency Act
CIPA   Children's Internet Protection Act
COPPA   Children's Online Privacy Protection Act
DMCA   Digital Millennium Copyright Act
E&IT   Ethics & Information Technology
EBM   Evidence-Based Medicine
EIT   Enhanced Interrogations and Torture
EU   European Union
FOIA   Freedom of Information Act
GPA   Grade Point Average
HIPAA   Health Insurance Portability and Accountability Act
ICIE   International Center for Information Ethics
ICT   Information and Communications Technology
IE   Information Ethics
IRE   Internet Research Ethics
IRIE   International Review of Information Ethics
JAMA   Journal of the American Medical Association
JIE   Journal of Information Ethics
MCAT   Medical College Admission Test
MOMA   Museum of Modern Art
MRI   Magnetic Resonance Imaging
NUCMC   National Union Catalog of Manuscript Collections

Introduction

The first mention of the term information ethics (IE) occurred in this author's 1988 *Ethical Challenges in Librarianship*; simultaneously, Rafael Capurro came up with *Informationsethik*. Four years later, I founded the *Journal of Information Ethics* (*JIE*), which I continue to edit. Capurro followed 12 years later with the *International Review of Information Ethics* (*IRIE*), an online publication based in Germany. And Martha Montague Smith decided to return to school to earn a second doctorate, invited me to serve on her committee as the outside advisor, and in 1996, at the University of North Carolina, wrote the first dissertation on the subject. I attended both her initial meeting and final oral exam.

Things progressed and IE caught on quite quickly in most disciplines; it is now an extremely diverse and broadly applied concept. It will strike some as curious but information and communication technologies (ICT), information technology, and computer ethics are all subsets of information ethics, which encompasses the production, dissemination, storage, access, retrieval, and application of information. The results of a general Google search for the ethics of information vary from four million to 12 million hits and for the exact phrase "Information Ethics," from 197,000 to 284,000 (both depending on the day that the search is done) and there are about 800 images, many of which are precisely appropriate.

It is obvious that informational benefits and pleasures are abundant; what the following study also shows is that informational flaws, harms, pathologies, and atrocities are equally ubiquitous. Smith's 1997 article presents an excellent summary and bibliographic overview of IE up to that point; her next piece, a 2001 overview, adds additional citations. Toni Carbo and Smith's 2008 piece bring things closer to the present moment and includes an extraordinarily replete bibliography of more than 400 items. See also the International Center for Information Ethics (ICIE) (http://icie.zkm.de/)—which is the parent of *IRIE*—for an overwhelming wealth of material on IE including news, hundreds of publications, and much more.

There is no need to rehearse the detailed historical or philosophical overviews of IE—its inception, development, manifestations, and influence—that Tom Froehlich and especially Jared Bielby, inter alios, have written. But a number of points bear noting. Bielby traces IE's conceptualization, if not its nominal demarcation, as far back as 1948 and Norbert Wiener's seminal work in cybernetics; he also claims that the term appeared prior to the present author's 1988 study. By 1990, courses in IE began to appear at the universities of Pretoria and Pittsburgh, as well as at Kent State (Bielby I). Computer ethics and cyberethics are but two areas where concerns of these disciplines strongly overlap with IE, and even UNESCO takes an interest in ethical applications of information.

Smith indicates that "the beginnings of information ethics are characterized by identifying the issues, establishing a vocabulary, and bringing both normative and non-normative analysis to bear..." (Smith, M. M. 340). Paul Sturges contends that the general center in informational discourse is shifting from an emphasis on technical matters to one in which ethics is emphasized and insinuates itself even into papers that ostensibly deal with technique. He discusses codes, books, journals, conferences, and education in order to show that information ethics is a powerful determining factor in the information and other professions.

Bielby observes that "The implications for an inclusive definition of Information Ethics are many, venturing into the realms of philosophical dialectics, metaphysics and hermeneutics..." (Bielby I) and this may be why ethicists have sometimes gone astray interpreting the concept too broadly or diversely or applying it where it has little relevance. Indeed, even those who have worked with it from its beginnings have extended its compass to, for example, global information justice, intercultural IE, or social action. The excellent publication *IRIE* devoted issues to "Global Digital Citizenship" and "Religion and IT" and the now apparently defunct *International Journal of Internet Research Ethics* contains "Creating a Web of Attribution in the Feminist Blogosphere." Naturally, more pointed journals such as *Ethics and Information Technology,* the *Journal of Medical Internet Research,* or the *Information Society* would logically include esoteric material that would less appropriately fall under the IE rubric (see listing of topics at end of this Introduction). Many scholars have devoted themselves to a lesser or greater extent to IE including Smith, Johannes Britz, Elizabeth Buchanan, Rafael Capurro, and especially Luciano Floridi, whose oeuvre is sometimes overwhelmingly theoretical, with little real world application.

Culture

At the same time, and to be fair when considering the remarkable expansion of IE boundaries, global or intercultural IE and global information justice are legitimate concepts that demand more than theoretical musing on the part of Americans or Europeans. Third World lives depend on literacy, technological skills, and access to information on "hunger, disease, poverty" (Smith, M. M. 355). As for the ethical treatment and use of information in a diversity of circumstances, what one may do and how this is accomplished vary dramatically in time and especially now in location. Different societies acculturate their peoples to correct action very differently. What is unobjectionable (if ostensibly illegal) in China or Thailand is unacceptable in the West, and one may pay a very high price—fine and imprisonment—for information piracy, for example. Ironically, what is unethical in most Western countries—libel, falsified information, trolling, hate speech, pornography—riddles the Internet. It is difficult to contend with the many cultural differences when faced with ethical problems.

It is easy to understand this when one recalls that corruption and bribes (baksheesh) are endemic (if illegal) in some lands and intolerable in others. Culture controls ethical decision-making, although even where cultural tradition appears to approbate certain (unethical) actions or policies, it is probable that individuals, organizations, government, and society all know that what is advocated is unacceptable, that is, wrong. In Ayi Kwei Armah's novel *The Beautyful Ones Are Not Yet Born,* the graft and corruption are counterbalanced by a single person with true integrity. His antipode can be found in Chinua Achebe's *No Longer at Ease* in which the fictional hero, knowing that bribery is wrong, nonetheless succumbs to the culturally acceptable but illegal practice.

Corruption, graft, and theft are not limited to fictional accounts. Even in countries where they are endemic and silently accepted, when they occur blatantly and when they ostensibly harm the nation in one way or another, they are found to be contemptible, and so it is the case in late 2016 in the Democratic Republic of Congo, where the president, Joseph Kabila, has stolen almost 100 million dollars from the government (Gettleman passim), that is, from the people, who should not have elected him in the first place. It will be difficult for cultural information ethicists to admit, but social practices are no excuse for bad, injurious behavior or actions.

Philip Brey's incisive discussion of the topic indicates how challenging it is to defend the present author's position. Brey shows how attitudes toward privacy, freedom of information, and intellectual property rights differ dramatically in the West from those in China, Japan, and Thailand. Mitigatingly, one can contend that historical referents may be less meaningful than Brey and others think, since, for example, a 2500 year old Confucian (or more recent Communist) attitude toward privacy has very little import in a world in which iPhones, Alibaba, and capitalistic tendencies have replaced traditional modalities, and where Western attitudes toward these concepts are undoubtedly slowly becoming acceptable.

History is not destiny. More compelling is European and American cultural and legal attitudes concerning privacy and freedom of speech. These two necessities clash and since only one can take precedence, a choice must be made. Europeans prefer privacy protection. So even here, minor cultural determinants in very similar social contexts do control ethical information policy.

The present author finds his own counter-argument disconcerting. Therefore, he will try a different tack. Under certain specific (historical) circumstances, it may be possible to defend *cultural* relativism and its diverse mores and accompanying taboos and the resulting shambles that infest global informational domains, where universalism (a consistent ethic) is necessary to avoid catastrophe. But because he is a Kantian deontologist, *ethical* relativism is indefensible. He holds that it does not matter where or when in humanity's lifespan an action occurs; some things are simply always right and others always wrong: It is always right to defend and protect the innocent, even if sometimes it is impossible to do so; it is *always* wrong to murder your close relatives and friends, to betray a trust, to cheat, dissimulate, and lie—before Sumer, in ancient China or Egypt, in Chichen Itza, in Nunavut, or in San Francisco. Naturally, one can come up with situations (scenarios) in which murdering your daughter or wife is preferable to global catastrophe, but such dilemmas occur more frequently in the minds of comfortably situated philosophers than in reality. Many people faced with such a horror would rather die. Human beings should grow up and stop causing harm! (The September 2010 issue of *IRIE* is allocated to intercultural information ethics.)

Problems

In a sadly telling sidelight, many years ago, this author observed to Martha Montague Smith, whose interest in the historical development of IE made her the logical person to inform, that the IE entry in *Wikipedia* was misleading and inaccurate. She responded with legitimate annoyance because it turned out that she was responsible for its creation. This was stunning and seemingly impossible. She subsequently took a look at the entry and discovered that what she had originally entered had been altered, deformed, or expunged by ideologues. This entry has now been revised again, probably on an ongoing basis, but it has given a false impression of IE, and is in itself an example of an ethical informational breach.

Or consider another real world problem, where theoretical musing means nothing and informationally ethical consideration and commitment would have forestalled a debacle. One of the world's most popular novelists, Elena Ferrante, has maintained absolute secrecy concerning her real identity. In late 2016, Claudio Gatti, an Italian journalist, basing his conclusions on financial records, revealed that she is probably Anita Raja. Loyal readers and others reacted negatively, condemning Gatti for breach of privacy, "sexist violation," and "unprovoked aggression" (Donadio). They are correct. If someone wishes to be an anonymous novelist, protective of his or her privacy (like Thomas Pynchon or J. D. Salinger), meddlers should mind their own business, especially here where anonymity is not protective of someone who is threatening or causing harm in any way.

Introduction

The (deontological) ethics controlling and determining information revelation mandates that one also take into account the harm that may occur to individuals or society. Gatti failed to consider anything other than his selfish objective. His revelation was a detriment.

Antithetically, *The New York Times'* publication of Donald Trump's 1995 tax return was a service to the public, which has the right to know something about the financial stability, honesty, and social commitment of a potential president, one who refused to indicate where he stands financially, although he brags about not paying taxes. Breaching privacy is ethically unacceptable, but shirking civic responsibility at this level augured very bad things for the nation. Trump's threatened libel suit would probably fail since this was "truthful information of public concern" (Liptak), unlike Gatti's revelation, which served no meaningful or useful purpose.

Because all human pursuits require, produce, and apply information, IE encompasses everything from academic disciplines to professions such as medicine and law, occupations, gaming, Internet searching and retrieval, and social media. Surprisingly, Richard Severson limits his discussion to just four principles (very different from Floridi's): respect for intellectual property, fair representation, privacy, and non-malfeasance, and these may be applied in many practical situations. But it is also necessary to set some boundaries and professional applications, censorship, privacy, access, digital life, and academia, inter alia, seem reasonable areas on which to concentrate. Entirely ignored in the present study are politics and legal ethics.

Data and information production or application are inherent in all sentient life and for 4,000 years humans have accumulated vast troves of information, orally and on or in tablets, scrolls, palm leaves, quipu, manuscripts, books, and computer servers, but they did not record all of the ephemeral detritus that accrued on a daily basis, so that much of the past's data are lost. And different civilizations treated their output differently. The ancient Egyptians recorded their thoughts on monuments in a lucidly clear hieroglyphic script. The Sumerians, on the other hand, secreted their cuneiform bills of lading, for example, in little, sealed, clay ampoules; in order to read what was recorded, the bottle, which had an affixed tag containing a description, had to be broken.

Introduction

It is possible that we now produce more data and information in a single day than was manufactured during all of recorded history. Much of this detritus is not merely ephemeral; it is sometimes potentially quite harmful: twitterings of text; children's photographs posted by their adoring parents; youngsters' and adolescents' inappropriate images and sextings; and vilely repugnant trollings. And all of the incessant cell phoning, allowing shopping husbands to ask their wives whether they need another watermelon, recorded by intelligence agencies, has many detrimental effects: it wastes electrical energy, causes people to sacrifice food and medicine in order to pay connection fees, and distorts and diminishes human and cultural interaction. One can only fearfully imagine how Neil Postman would react now, three decades after publishing *Amusing Ourselves to Death*, to our brave new world of the Internet, Facebook, and ubiquitous cellphones.

The extent of all of this may be measured by a simple personal observation: my young teenage daughter has 20,000 images on her computer, 50,000 songs that she purchased or acquired legally, and access, naturally, to countless additional musical compositions. Every week, she produces and receives thousands of emails and especially texts, most of which have little or no value. She begins this process as she awakes, while lying in bed, and continues incessantly creating vast troves of data and information. She has taken 60,000 self images that she has disseminated via Snapchat; two of her friends are at the 200,000 mark. (In just a few months since first written these numbers have increased to 92,000 and 270,000 respectively; these teenagers are in competition to have very high counts.) She is never without her cell phone and desires a new one each time a new version of the iPhone appears. It is an extraordinary waste of time to spend five or ten hours a day on a mobile device; this is similar to spending half of every day watching television.

Data and information should be dealt with in an ethical and legal manner, but they are not. Rogues create databases (Library Genesis, BookZZ, Sci-Hub) of stolen books and journal articles, and legitimate, ostensibly honest people avail themselves of the material, perhaps excusing themselves because they desperately need something. Big greedy companies such as Elsevier take advantage of everyone, which apparently allows the upstanding to condone theft. Bryn Geffert, the Amherst College librarian, makes a case for Sci-Hub's piracy: "Nobody who needs scholarship should go without" and "It is immoral to deny information to those who need it" (B4, B5). Free access to all information is not the human *right* she claims it to be, despite the United Nations Declaration, which, in any case, is a more general statement (see Chapter 13).

Geffert's argument is not very convincing, since it is both unethical and illegal to steal anything, including information, no matter how worthy the objective, no matter how exploitative the big publishing companies may be. If a bank steals one's house through a fraudulent loan and an unjust foreclosure, it is highly inadvisable to rob its tellers at gunpoint claiming turnabout is fair play. And it is unnecessary, despite Geffert's assertion, that one must offer "a credible alternative" to theft in order to insist that what this site does is unethical as are the actions of those who misuse its content.

So, along comes a good idea: open access will counter the high cost of journal subscriptions, except, naturally, that the author must pay as much as $3,100 to publish an article either in excellent legitimate periodicals or in predatory journals. All this does is shift the cost from one entity to another, in this case, one that is far less likely to have a large endowment upon which to draw. (See Peekhaus.) Google Books is similar but because the company is so powerful, it gets away with this same kind of (partial) theft. Even writers defend it, but not all. The Authors' Guild lost a suit against Google Books and the Supreme Court refused to take on the case. Project Gutenberg is different; it includes out of copyright material, so— like Dover which reprints old volumes and sells them inexpensively— Gutenberg provides a service and does not harm through theft, although it does harm bookstores which sell fewer copies of the novels of Jane Austen, since she sits atop the lists of chosen authors. Millions of people make use of this free service, either reading online or downloading material. Those who think that this is an extraordinary boon, might reconsider the public library. (See also the Aaron Swartz case in Chapter 13.)

Predatory journals, those that exist only to earn money for their publishers and do not provide real editorial vetting, prey on both the naive and those who know that they are being scammed but desperately need another publication and presumably hope that peers and administrators do not follow up and discover that their venue is not a legitimate publication.

Introduction

Misinformation, factual distortion, and outright deception are rampant not only in cyberspace, but also in the real world: Donald Trump has shown that it is possible to convince people even when they know he is lying. And propagandists continue to spew out purposely false information. Russia specializes in producing disinformation to confuse and harm. Credulous people believe almost anything: The evidence in evidence-based medicine is without merit to the true believer who knows that prayer or homeopathy will cure a horrific disease.

The following work offers a comprehensive overview and analysis of and normative adjurations in many of the disciplines and areas where IE has an influential role to play, where ethical commitment to every aspect of information and informatics may successfully precede the intervention of draconian law; when all else fails and human beings refuse to act decently or ethically, the law impinges. The European Union (EU) levies a 100 million Euro fine on organizations that refuse to follow the dictates of its 1995 Data Protection Directive, which mandates (demands) the right to be forgotten. (See *LearnTechLib,* a site that brings together 77 papers and other documents on information ethics with an emphasis on education.)

The *International Journal of Technoethics* presents an extreme example of the multiplication of related topics covered in its pages:

Artificial morality	Environmental technoethics
Biomedical ethics	Ethics and autonomous agents
Biotech ethics	Ethics and cloning
Codes of technoethics	Ethics and e-health
Communication ethics	Ethics and e-learning
Computer ethics	Ethics and genetic doping
Cyber democracy	Ethics and genetic programming
Cyber-bullying	Ethics and technological systems
Cybercrime and corruption	Ethics and telemedicine
Cyberethics cyber pornography	Fertilization
Cyber-stalking	Historical technoethics
Digital Divide	Identity theft in vitro
Digital property ethics	Information ethics
E-business ethics	Internet ethics
Educational technoethics	Inter-organizational technoethics
Engineering ethics	Laws of technoethics

Introduction

Management technoethics
Media Ethics
Military technoethics
Nanoethics
Netiquette neuroethics
Nuclear ethics
Organizational technoethics
Privacy
Professional technoethics
Software piracy
Spam
Sport technoethics
Spyware
Technoethical theory
Technoethics and art
Technoethics and biometrics
Technoethics and cognitive studies
Technoethics and computer-mediated communication
Technoethics and culture
Technoethics and decision making
Technoethics and design

Technoethics and digital governance
Technoethics and globalization
Technoethics and human computer interaction
Technoethics and human rights
Technoethics and information systems
Technoethics and instructional systems
Technoethics and knowledge management
Technoethics and law
Technoethics and online communities
Technoethics and poverty
Technoethics and religion
Technoethics and science
Technoethics and security
Technoethics and social theory
Technoethics and society
Technoethics and technology studies
Technoethics and urban studies
Technoethics and work
Technoethics of war and violence
Technology abuse

1 Data and Information

It is extremely difficult to know with certitude—and it is of course the task of parents and educators to teach and inculcate modes of discovery—ways in which critical acumen can help developing children learn to make valid assessments (although, naturally, a great deal of inherent belief and propaganda confuse the malleable). This, in essence, is the task of epistemology, if a practical task may be assigned to a philosophical discipline. Here one learns how one knows and how one knows that what one knows is valid. There are reasonable and logical tests for these things and an overview of epistemological rudiments makes this lucidly clear. Here, let it suffice to alert readers, who may be dismayed, that a very high percentage of everything they *know* to be true derives not from personal empirical experience but rather from social, cultural, religious, political, historical, and scientific authority. Sometimes these sources are incorrect.

Data

Data comprise numbers, statistics, and straightforward facts. Data without context are meaningless. It is analogous to written Arabic, where words consist exclusively of consonants; vowels are only included in children's books and the Koran. So even a native speaker comprehends only 75 percent of what is offered from the text; the other 25 percent derives from context. Sometimes no data on a subject are available at all. Small amounts of data comprise insignificant personal or global factoids, meaningful only to a limited group of people unless applied to an individual by a marketer in order to sell something, which in a more caring world would be considered unethical. And it is as if a company such as Target or Mother Frockers (formerly, a real New York business) contacts a young girl with solicitations for maternity items because something she purchased for her aunt implied that she was pregnant, though she was only 11 and not. This can be avoided by not using store lagniappes or credit cards, buying online, or in extreme cases even using Visa, MasterCard, or Discover, or divulging personal data in any way. But this is very difficult to do, and because of human nature for many people who do not consider matters, and offer their social security numbers to anyone who asks, impossible. For example, airlines seduce customers into loyalty programs by offering meaningless upgrades or free flights after one accumulates 10 million miles. Few people actually profit from these programs and customers would be much better off with less expensive initial costs.* Corporations, government agencies, and most other large entities are now engaged in the datafication of their processes.

The concept of Big Data is agglomerated from hundreds of thousands or millions of anonymous individual data points and then applied in order to accomplish many things by allowing humans or computers to make swift and accurate decisions. Such big data are especially beneficial to marketers who try to sell their products to an ever increasing constituency, but it is also applicable and useful in banking, health care, education, and other areas where data play a meaningful role, for example, any occurrence that trends in a specific direction such as the incidence of an illness or crime or a product's increasing sales. But they are also very dangerous, as Cathy O'Neill shows in *Weapons of Math Destruction.* They are impenetrable, operate in an extremely large sphere, and can cause human harm, because they are sometimes misleading—in finance, educational evaluation, and college admissions (Shirky).

Vu Le discusses serious problems and reminds readers that data are

---

*Loyalty programs are notorious for denying miles for many reasons, blocking people on specific days, and not having any available seats. When this author's wife and he flew around the world, each quickly accumulating some 30,000 miles, United gave each of them credit for less than 8,000, which were never redeemed and thus lost. Despite the many hundreds of flights he has taken, he has received only one free trip. His wife's and daughter's equally enormous number of flights have resulted in absolutely nothing, except safe arrivals.

sometimes not objective, valid, or generalizable; they simplify matters; accountability results in blaming; data hoard resources, act as a gatekeeper, are imperfect, and pathologize communities. Data can be de-weaponized by contextualization, payment, disaggregation, and additional possibilities explored in this incisive blog post (Le passim).

Information

Information is codified data, and it is through this codification that they come to have meaning and import. When a body of information is formulated and structured into a foundational gestalt, the basis for a discipline such as chemistry or linguistics, for example, it transcends into knowledge. Data as incipient information and information as the basis for a knowledge base both, naturally, also exist within an ethical environment.

Here is a real-life example. A datum is the fact that a normal blood pressure for a healthy American adult is about 120 over 70. Naturally, considerably lower or higher numbers are still within an acceptable range. Using or applying this datum to the fact that as blood pressure decreases or increases dramatically, very bad things happen including loss of consciousness, heart attack, stroke, and death, comprises an informational packet. Medical practitioners are privy to additional information concerning blood pressure: how and why it works, what causes problems, how to resolve them, and so on. All of this plus cognizance of human anatomy and physiology generally, and arterial strength, histological function, and hundreds of other processes, specifically, form the partial foundation of biological function—the knowledge base for human molecular biology and its medical derivations and applications. Ignoring, misusing, or abusing this knowledge is an ethical breach, often manifested by the person whose pressure is abnormal.

One may legitimately wonder whether there is anything to say about information that is not obvious or that has not already been explored. James Gleick thought so and in 2011, he published *The Information: A History, a Theory, a Flood,* 500 pages of informational inquiry. Very sadly but not surprisingly, neither ethical considerations nor even scientific misconduct turn up here. What Gleick does offer is a history of informational communication—from talking drums to telegraphy, telephony, and so

---

on—and a theoretical examination of technical information and the technologies that support it—from Charles Babbage (and his Difference Engine), Norbert Wiener, and Alan Turing to Claude Shannon's theorizing in his seminal *Mathematical Theory of Communication*, and much else that views the term in a very different light; this is a scientific not a philosophical theory of information. In this expanded sense, everything is informational including genetic codes and black holes.

Quantum information complicates matters and lots of very important physicists turn up including Maxwell and Gamow, Wheeler and Hawking, most of whom the man and woman on the street, though familiar with information in its multitudinous guises, never encountered, unless they had studied physics. What one discovers here is that information is never destroyed (358). This is a bit like the physicist's pronouncement that time travel is not impossible. This author disagrees with both contentions, since much of the past's local and extraterrestrial information is gone forever (and we are not going back to retrieve it); some of these theorizers do not even know their great-grandparents' names. In the theoretical (Floridian) infosphere (323), which Gleick mentions but which is not included in the index, entropy (uncertainty concerning messages due to noise) (289) is the key to understanding information but not necessarily its meaning, because sometimes, according to Shannon, there is none, since it has no relevance to engineering (416). And this esoteric theorizing is of no concern to information ethicists.

What does matter is what the onslaught of information means for the information society. Richard Cox observes that we are inundated with advertisements and demands for our attention and money for every new technological device and implementation but things have not only not gotten easier, we now inhabit an electronic sweatshop where we must be connected at all times and are thereby dehumanized (53, 55). His solution is a return to spirituality leading to religious redemption (60, 62), though this neither mitigates nor replaces our dependence on IT nor would this work for or help most people.

Data-derived information is ubiquitous and necessary for the propagation and enhancement of all sentient life. Is it necessary to delineate this? Honey bees thrive because of the information gleaned through discovery and then communicated by dance to their fellow hive-mates. It is possible to analyze information from a philosophical, sociological, psychological, or economic perspective and in all of these cases the theoretical may jibe with the practical but it also may clash, sometimes diametrically. All of these approaches are touched upon in this study, but not in the sometimes exquisite detail that scholars have applied in their limited disciplines, exemplified by Max Weber's *Protestant Ethic and the Spirit of Capitalism*, Kenneth Arrow's *Economics of Information*, or Fritz Machlup's *Knowledge: Its Creation, Distribution and Economic Significance*, in ten projected volumes!

There exist three classes of information.

1. *Public*, which encompasses what anyone might discover or know: that which is observable in nature or in the manufactured world of human beings: rain forests or facts, articulated thought, gossip—everything available anywhere.

2. *Private*, which is inadvertently or purposely concealed from others. Here is included what one does in private; what one thinks or believes that is not shared with others; personal matters such as illness, finances, affairs, crimes—things that are no one else's business, but which upon revelation have only minimally negative effects, but devastating enough.

3. *Secret*, which can be of a personal, corporate, or governmental nature. Individuals do hold sensitive secrets the divulgement of which would result in irrevocable harm. A reasonable example is the person safeguarded in the witness protection program. Businesses have trade secrets, such as Coca-Cola's formula, the betrayal of which would cause financial loss. Most critical are national secrets that protect a country and its citizens from military incursion, hacking, and terrorism; some would also include political machination here, but it is often so sordid that it does not deserve consideration. (See also Chapters 12 and 13.) All types of information can be used and applied in an ethical manner or abused to cause harm.

Surprisingly, sometimes public information is kept secret. (See Chapter 9 for remarks on government control and Chapter 13 for secret law, the one thing that should never remain undisclosed.)

There is far too much data and information available, something that David Shenk noted 20 years ago. We are inundated, buried under our own detritus, far more now then in 1997, since the Internet has evolved and social media have exploded. We know lots of useless things but the really critical information is lost to us. In the past we could quickly repair a defective automobile or radio or fly a small plane. Try fixing a computer controlled Mercedes or piloting a 747! Much worse, according to Byung-Chul Han, is the negative effect of Twitter and Facebook communication which is "responsible for the disintegration of community and public space" and negates true political interaction. The communicators are fragmented and harm individuals and "information has overrun thought."

Misinformation

Misinformation is the scourge of the information society generally, and the digital age more precisely. Indeed, it is the Internet and the broad and deep cyberworld that it reveals for anyone anywhere that allows so much rubbish to accumulate and confuse. During the past decade, there have appeared a host of monographic studies that clarify, advise, and suggest how to confront and overcome misinformation (see Helfand's, Sarokin's, and Levitin's studies in the bibliography). Misleading, deceptive, and patently false information derive from many sources some of which are innocuous while others are extremely harmful. Here are five possibilities. They all defy truth.

1. *Inadvertent error* occurs when one mistakes a claim for a fact, an inaccurate idea for a truth, an integer for its neighbor, a computation or procedure for its antithesis. Minor errors can sneak into otherwise factual narratives or accurate calculations: A wrong date, misspelled name, confused location, or mathematical mistake is easy to indicate but often difficult to correct, especially if it occurs in a published citation, a not uncommon occurrence. On October 7, 2016, *The New York Times* published a little map of central Israel. The scale indicated that half an inch is equal to 150 miles. This is off by a factor of exactly 11, and so the 34 mile straight-line distance between Tel Aviv and Jerusalem appears to be 375. This minor error could have a devastating effect. Prior to the Internet, hard copy publishers scrupulously edited texts for accuracy; *The New Yorker* is notorious for its fact checking; *The New York Times* publishes a compilation of corrections in each day's paper. There is no way that everything everyone indicates can be factually perfect. Error is so prevalent

that in physics, for example, after an experiment is performed, one does an error analysis.

Error calculation also takes place in polling where accuracy is indicated "with a margin of error of three percent in either direction." (In the latter instance, it is probable that the margin often may be much greater—especially in cases where the prediction does not come to pass!) The Internet altered the way in which material is vetted for truth. Much that is propagated here is mistaken simply because no one bothered to verify a definition or claim or belief or narrative or image or email message or text. And search engine algorithms can produce misleading or faulty data and information (Noble). Additionally, self-published books, which have proliferated greatly during the past decade or two, may lack careful external editing and fact checking.

An extraordinary personal experience offers a blatant example of the frequency and potential harm of mistaken information due to error. The present author has nine separate health insurance policies for himself and his family (not by choice). He requires ocular injections (perhaps as many as 12 per year) each of which costs $4,000. The company that produces the medicine indicated that Medicare and Blue Cross would pay and this the representatives stated on two separate occasions; the doctor's billing specialist stated unequivocally that the cost is covered; on the other hand both Medicare and Blue Cross indicated that it is not. All of this was communicated telephonically. Two of these four entities are mistaken and have miscommunicated important information. (It turned out that the cost is covered.) We have become a global nation of inadvert misstaters.

A special class of error occurs when ostensibly accurate data are misapplied because a plethora of competent (scientific) bureaucrats fail to consider every angle. The results can be devastating. Consider data and information that seem to imply that a first nuclear strike is underway. Those responsible for a counter-attacking defense could react precipitously and mistakenly and the result might be devastation or annihilation (see the film *WarGames)*. Human beings are far too immature to be responsible for nuclear and biological weaponry. A superb real-life example of the misapplication of incontrovertible data is the series of simulations done in *Sully,* the film that explores and details the extraordinary 2009 Hudson River plane landing executed by Chesley Sullenberger. For virtually everyone, Sullenberger was an unmitigated hero, but government bureaucrats had to investigate and the Federal Aviation Administration and the National Transportation Safety Board attempted to show that an airport landing was feasible. This they did by running simulations, but the data were incomplete, and the simulations failed to simulate reality. The film dramatizes the way in which this is foiled but in essence it is correct—and all 155 people on board were saved. It is highly probable that Sullenberger would have failed to make it back to Laguardia or to Teteboro in New Jersey and a crash would have resulted in 155 deaths and inconceivable damage on the ground. Additionally, had this misapplication of erroneous data not been caught, it could have destroyed Sullenberger's career. (See *Sully 2016. History vs Hollywood* for a superb and replete comparison of what actually occurred and the cinematic interpretation.)

Once an error is recognized, and especially if one is accused, there exist five possible responses and Brian Martin discusses each of these in detail: First, one may decide to simply ignore the error, that is, cover it up; second, it is possible to "counter-attack" an accuser; third, one may offer a reinterpretation of the material; fourth, an "acknowledgment in context" is an honorable solution; and fifth, most obvious, and very difficult for many people, is an "unqualified apology" (35–39). Errors can be damaging; they should be corrected, if at all possible, and this despite the bog of untruthfulness into which politics has sunk.

2. *Misplaced belief* is probably the primary source for the inundation of misinformation that confuses humankind, and the primary cause is religion which encompasses an astonishing array of possibilities, from the beliefs and practices of animists and pantheists and ancient peoples such as the Aztecs and Egyptians to the major contemporary faiths: Judaism, Christianity, Islam, Hinduism, Buddhism, Taoism, and Shinto. There are many other (minor) manifestations including Hare Krishna, Scientology, Wicca, and New Age. (For a complete overview see "The Big Religion Chart" in the Bibliography.) Religion propagates and necessitates belief in unquestionable dogma. These beliefs are often diametrically opposed to each other and in discord with reality. Humans, unlike their close animal brothers, require something to give their lives meaning, hope, and cultural community, and parents pass down religious commitment to their offspring who, with very few exceptions, find it difficult to disabuse them-

selves of their religious heritage. The more orthodox the parents, the more difficult is apostasy. Only a tiny percentage of human beings reject one religion in order to embrace another. When a religious precept clashes with reality, the committed simply reject the latter. Another bizarre tactic that the sophisticated implement is to divide matters in such a way that they do not seem to clash, so that a physicist with a stake in nature and its laws will insist that science and religion serve different purposes and thus different masters (nature and god), which hardly solves the problems of intelligent design, evolution, or global warming.

Religion is but the apex of misplaced belief. Here is also located the convictions of those who work in what might be termed the soft, predictive disciplines, those unlike chemistry, which can indicate with absolute accuracy what will occur when taconite is alloyed with a five percent nickel admixture. The results do not vary. Economists cannot even agree on what caused the Great Depression or if inflation or deflation is better for the economy, and their decisions are sometimes quite detrimental, which does not alter their faith in whatever ideology propels them. The Federal Reserve has for a decade maintained extremely low interest rates holding that this will boost a sagging economy, while one fifth of the population has suffered on fixed incomes, social security paycheck to paycheck. Political scientists also have a controlling set of beliefs, which often turn out to be misplaced. Fascism, communism, socialism, and capitalism cannot all be equally valid, but convincing true believers that there is something radically wrong with their commitment is impossible.

Some outlandish literary theorists hold that the author of a work is no more qualified to interpret its meaning than any arbitrarily chosen reader, perhaps one who never encountered a novel, and so knows nothing of its history or conventions or anything about nineteenth century culture or Dickens, who, say, wrote *Oliver Twist.* (One should not confuse this position with the less extreme intentional fallacy.) This imaginary reader's interpretation is just as valid as Dickens', that of the scholar who has devoted 40 years to his work, and the doctoral candidate in Victorian literature. This hardly seems reasonable. Theoreticians sometimes allow themselves to propagate nonsense.

Metricians believe and have convinced others that value can be assigned based on the frequency of scholarly attributions garnered from citations. Alberto Bartoli and Eric Medvet insist that "ease of web discovery, ease of access, and content relevance rather than quality influence what gets read and cited ... [and] research evaluation based on citation counts works against many types of high-quality works" (abstract). Metrics are probably less meaningful than proponents think. Nevertheless, they are used to control academic careers. Even worse is the more recent administrative dependence on "inaccurate and insufficient" data derived from faculty performance that is individually agglomerated and then fed back to institutions by Academic Analytics, a commercial concern. This is so unpalatable that faculty have rebelled and subscribing schools have canceled their agreements. The original goal was to rid the institutions of low performing professors. This has changed but it is still a nasty business (Basken).

By early 2018, things had degenerated to such a degree that Jefferson Pooley makes a strong case against Academia.edu, a researchers' social-network company, similar to ResearchGate, that attempts to quantify the quality of a scholar's output. Administrators monitor employees' records but individuals are also seduced into checking constantly to see how many people are reading or citing their work. Pooley notes that "The site has grown rapidly by preying on scholars' hunger for visibility" (B4). He further suggests that scholars cease to cooperate with these commercial entities and implies that we diminish our own interest in metrical evaluations (B5). (See below for additional discussion.)

And, finally, here must be appended self-deception and the many crackpot theories that seem valid to their proponents but are not. The Chapman University poll of Americans shows that 46.6 percent believe in haunting spirits; 27 percent think that visitors from outer space have arrived on earth; big foot is and Atlantis was real; 54.3 percent indicate that the government knows something it is not revealing about 9/11 and 49.6 percent think the same thing about JFK's assassination (Poppy 16, 17). People are misinformed, gullible, and believe what they want to believe.

3. *Statistical manipulation* is ubiquitous, even if perpetrated unwittingly. But naturally most people who wish to convince someone that something is so will manipulate the statistic or the manner in which it is offered. It is easy to lie using numbers, and depending on how the data

are presented, one can indicate almost anything. Even the raw results of statistical calculation (central tendency) and tests (chi-square, t-test, ANOVA, multiple regression, and so on) can be purposely deceptive depending on what has been input and how the results are presented. The same criticism can be levied against graphing, maps, and—less directly relevant in this context but connected substantively—manipulated images of, for example, photographs, astronomical bodies, cell cultures, bacteria, or proteins, which alter the impact of the accompanying text in favor of the hypothesis, discussion, or argument. (See Chapter 19.)

More than half a century ago, Darrell Huff published *How to Lie with Statistics*, which many years later inspired Mark Monmonier to do the same thing for cartography. His *How to Lie with Maps* is revelatory. And these led to many other "how to lie with" works including big and bad data and visualization. Apparently, though, it is not necessary to learn to lie when it comes to social media; here, all one must do is prevaricate and the gullible will believe individuals' remarks or opinions or fake news from sites and feeds.

Sampling, in one form or another, is the social scientist's major weapon. It is based on weak foundational theory and often results in false conclusions, as the Trump triumph clearly shows. This is because it is postulated that 1500 randomly chosen people are a reliable and valid representation of the entire U.S. population. Nielsen ratings derived from just 5,000 households (14,000 and even 50,00 are also hypothetically mentioned) presumably watching television control entire industries. What if the TV set is on but no one is at home? what if people choose programs based on their participation in the Nielsen program so that they watch PBS rather than the Playboy channel? and what if all of those Nielsen households are tuned in to the news that John F. Kennedy was assassinated (to make a disconnected, ahistorical jump), but most of America's viewers are actually watching *SpongeBob SquarePants*? Sampling and polling often offer distorted, misleading statistical data.

4. *Purposeful distortion* occurs when speakers or writers either hold a false idea or know that what they propagate is incorrect but do not care because they have a higher agenda to further or because they wish to cause harm for its own sake. Lee McIntyre, in *Respecting Truth*, observes that ideological organizations—"...cable news channels, advocacy groups, think

tanks, political campaigns, and industry research groups..."—impersonate media and the academy in order to further their doctrinaire beliefs (95). Some of what is published in the traditional manner and much of what one finds on the Internet is purposely false including "deceptive apps" and "fake news." Facebook has produced so much of this rubbish, which has had a negative effect on international politics, for example, that it, Google, and some governments are doing something about it. Paul Mozur and Mark Scott provide many examples of blatantly falsified news reports (A1, B4). (See also http://yournewswire.com/). Melissa Zimdars created a list of sites that present unreliable material; she also offers tips to help people assess the validity of news sites (Dreid).

The gullible believe, but these deceptions are usually, though not always, clear to the knowledgeable in specific fields or those who can critically analyze blatant propaganda (which deceives through unfair emphasis, exaggeration, and misdirection) and abjure its influence. But there exists an unusual category of distorted material that is difficult or impossible for the nonspecialist to evaluate. Here, an author begins with precise factual material acceptable to almost every knowledgeable scholar in the appropriate field (history, anthropology, physics) and builds a reasonable and logical case or argument. But then subtly, peculiar or unwarranted or misinterpreted or falsified notions begin to sneak in until eventually the validity of the entire argument is vitiated. When this type of work is especially acute, it becomes the obsession of a conspiracist or crackpot. There exists a physical museum of hoaxes (see hoaxes.org); it offers details on purposeful deceptions throughout the course of human history.

Perhaps the most egregious case here is Holocaust denial. The Holocaust was the single worst purposeful, designed, and executed disaster in human history, worse in import, suffering, and result than Napoleon's rampages, the two world wars, or the Russian and Chinese revolutions, among the many other evil misdeeds of the psychopathic. Raw numbers are not the determining factor, though the numbers are certainly astounding; the death of even a single human being is cause for sadness, but this heinous genocide perpetrated by German fascists murdered six million Jews and five million other innocent victims including disabled Germans, Polish citizens, Jehovah's Witnesses, Roma, homosexuals, and others, 11 million human beings in all, and this does not take into account the civilians and military personnel maimed and killed. The evidence and proof of the transport, mistreatment, torture, and murder of these people is incontrovertible: photographs, films, survivors and liberators (both of whom this author has encountered), eyewitness accounts, historical and business records, various surviving camps, German reparations, and the missing people, whose relatives in distant countries continue to mourn their destruction. It is an ethical breach of demented proportions to deny all of this and claim that the Holocaust is a myth.

Holocaust denial helps to affirm anti–Semitism and riles any decent person who learns of its existence. It was widespread enough for Deborah Lipstadt to publish *Denying the Holocaust; The Growing Assault on Truth and Memory* in 1993. David Irving, a notorious Holocaust denier, filed a libel suit against her and her publisher in a British court, where one must prove innocence rather than guilt, that is, Lipstadt had to prove that the Holocaust occurred rather than that Irving had to show it was a myth, something that would be impossible to do (it is impossible to *prove* a negative). This was a travesty of judicial proceedings and it is repugnant that the civil court system in a civilized country would have the audacity to force a renowned and respected scholar to prove that a historical event occurred. It as if a lunatic sued Samuel Eliot Morison for claiming that Henry Hudson, among many other European explorers, sought the Northwest Passage. Information ethics is breached so egregiously here that Irving should have had to pay in some meaningful way for his attack. He did: He lost his home. Subsequently, Lipstadt wrote a follow-up study and Mick Jackson directed *Denial,* a film of this travesty with a screenplay by David Hare and starring Rachel Weisz.

A penultimate example can be found in traditional book reviews, where it is not so blatant, but nevertheless present, and in online reviews of books but also products and services. Here, in all of these instances, individuals exaggerate, distort, or lie. Most egregious are those ostensibly objective positive comments but written by the book's author, friends, or hired ghost-writers. Incredibly, there are numerous ethical problems associated with book reviewing and they are covered in detail in a special issue of the *Journal of Information Ethics* ("Ethical"). With services, if a person had a difficult time, he or she might say vilely offensive things in order to punish a maladroit plumber.

Finally, the Western capitalist economy revolves around and derives much of its potency from something that is taken for granted and is only criticized when it has a direct, immediate, and often personal effect; that is, it harms or annoys or seduces, especially children. This is the enormous and powerful world of advertising where print and online ads bombard readers and viewers and television commercials have become so over-whelmingly frequent and oppressive that many people delete or ignore them, even when they might prove beneficial. See Chapter 15 for a detailed discussion.

It is also possible to come at distortion from an entirely different per-spective and that is what a group of authors do in A. J. Angulo's *Miseducation*, a collection of essays that highlights the defiance of informational validity through discussions of purposeful, intentional, socially con-structed ignorance, uncaring, dispiriting, denigrating, and unethical for its abrogation of one's right to know the truth—about, for example, "tobacco, asbestos, and climate change" (Angulo, "Ignorance" 5). Consider that some of the Confederate states, as early as 1740, passed draconian laws that forbade teaching slaves to read or write thus maintaining igno-rance (Tolley 13–14) and thereby controlling not merely their access to information but their freedom. Other areas where ignorance is fostered include sex, evolution, and the environment (Angulo, *Miseducation* pas-sim). Here is how the sophisticated confuse the gullible:

> The Cato Institute, a partisan think tank, has recently published *"Silent Spring" at 50: The False Crisis of Rachel Carson*, a work that has the hallmarks of meta-agnotology [the study of ignorance]. The book's self-described aim is to expose and analyze "a number of Carson's major arguments [, which] rested on what can only be described as deliberate ignorance." In its quest to expose ignorance production in Carson's *Silent Spring*, the Cato Study has left in its wake a trail of controversy for the following: the financial connection between *"Silent Spring" at 50* and a Libertarian organization funded by such corporate giants as Philip Morris, R. J. Reynolds, Chevron, Exxon, Shell, the American Petroleum Institute, Eli Lilly, Merck, and Pfizer; the timing of the book's publication to coincide with fiftieth-anniversary celebrations of Carson's groundbreaking book; the aim of creating doubts about Carson's research, which has inspired generations of mainstream scientists and ecologists; the role of business, law, and economics professors rather than scientists in editing a volume about sci-ence; and the longstanding tradition of distorting the historical, scientific, and policy record surrounding Carson to advance what appear to be contemporary regulatory interests [Angulo "Reflections" 345].

1. Data and Information

This work will have a deleterious effect especially in education. "... [T]he Cato Institute is on the cutting edge of using agnotological analysis for the purpose of ignorance-making" (Angulo, "Reflections 345). This is always the case with think tanks (regardless of political persuasion), which exist, like lobbyists, to promulgate and disseminate their specific points of view but which are very frequently reactionary, propagandized, and full of patently false nonsense. Think of the Heartland Institute, which creates glossy brochures and other means "proving" that tobacco is harmless and climate change a myth.

Michiko Kakutani indicates that Tom Nichols' recent study, *The Death of Expertise*, is a fairly good summary of the new attitude toward knowledge and fact: anti-intellectualism, unreason, and acceptance of the nonsense promulgated on and disseminated via the Internet are ubiquitous. She notes that Al Gore's *Assault on Reason* and Susan Jacoby's *Age of American Unreason*, among other titles, present a fuller picture.

5. *Disinformation* is an extreme and purposeful form of informational distortion that broadcasts untruth. It may derive from a movement or organization but especially from a government that wishes to confuse and cause harm. In perverted form it is what one finds Winston Smith perpetrating in *1984*, as he alters the historical record at the Ministry of Truth (Orwell). The current Russian administration under Vladimir Putin is notorious for its disinformation program aimed at convincing the world that his country is good and kind and caring and its enemies (including, once again, the United States) are evil and harmful. In the spring of 2016, two U.S. Senators authored a bill to counter disinformation programs emanating from any country but especially China and Russia (Philipp W4). (It should be noted that propaganda is not necessarily false, but will exaggerate a biased position.) Russia is currently deploying facsimile weaponry in order to fool its enemies (and perhaps impress its friends). These planes, tanks, and other equipment are made of a strong fabric and are inflated or deflated at a moment's notice. This is part of a larger program that employs trickery and deception in order to win military encounters (Kramer). These balloon-like weapons may be scary but probably not all that effective in the long run. And so, IE has a hard task ahead; even the U.S. government is responsible for inundating its own citizens with purposeful informational distortion: Trumpian truthful hyperbole, post-truth,

alternative facts, and fake news contaminate the media and cyberspace and it takes a real commitment to ferret out what is truly valid. Many people do not care.

Counterknowledge may be considered a sophisticated form of disinformation. It is either produced by a true believer or purposely created by someone who favors conspiracies and crackpot ideas. If enough people come to believe and accept that the earth is really flat, that alligators inhabit New York City's sewers, that Barack Obama was not born in the U.S., that Lyndon Baines Johnson had President Kennedy killed, that ten-dimensional strings undergird the universe, that neuroscientific research provides apodictic evidence that free will does not exist, then the false conceptions metamorphose into "facts." Everywhere, but especially in cyberspace, it is often difficult to ascertain what is valid and what is drivel.

2   Ethics and Law

Ethics

Historically, ethical commitment precedes legal mandate. Early hominids did not have a codified set of rules that controlled their actions. They acted instinctively in order to survive and to ensure the survival of their kin, clan, or tribe. Taboos controlled their actions (as they often do for contemporary humans, who are chary of admitting it) and they knew what was right and good for them. Those who misbehaved were ostracized, banned, or killed. This orients the origin and evolution of ethics, that branch of philosophy which deals with acceptable, correct, and good action; ideally, what a person ought to do not because of threat or fear but because it is the right thing; one should do the deed for its own sake, so that one does not steal data from an employer because theft is wrong and socially unacceptable, for many reasons, and not because one may be embarrassed or fired or arrested.

When ethical admonition fails, the law takes over. Since humans cannot be trusted to adhere to the ethical imperative that theft is wrong and when the theft is particularly egregious, those responsible for instituting legal controls take a defensibly draconian position. So, that is why armed robbery of a postal employee is punishable by a 25 year sentence in federal prison. This ostensibly stops thieves from harming a postal employee or stealing first class mail, which may contain invaluable, irreplaceable documents such as bearer bonds or deeds or passports or citizenship papers. I do doubt that an analogous theft of a United Parcel or Federal Express package would have the same result. Indeed, it is possible that the perpetrator would avoid imprisonment.

The Scope of Information Ethics

There are many potential bases and ways in which ethical decisions can be made, and philosophers are notorious for compounding and complexifying matters, circling around these possibilities from every conceivable angle and then repeating things with slight variations ad nauseam. This allows academics to write and publish and thereby achieve recognition and tenure, but much of it is really superfluous. Matters can be boiled down to three basic modalities, the structure of which has been covered by various religions' holy books, Aristotle's *Nichomachean Ethics*, Kant's *Fundamental Principles of the Metaphysics of Morals*, Bentham's and Mill's posturing, and a handful of other works. All the rest is pilpul. Either one acts because it is the right thing to do, and one knows this because of religious or cultural or personal experience—and this is Kant's deontological demand to do one's duty, and for the present author, it is the primary means of effecting an ethically tenable outcome—or one is admonished to act in accordance with the potential results of his or her actions; this is Bentham's and Mill's consequentialism.

But the ends never justify the means. Thus, some people would refuse survival in Auschwitz and others are aghast that the U.S. government manipulated legalities in order to justify torturing fellow human beings, no matter how egregiously heinous their acts, no matter what the consequences might have been, and no matter what horrors might have been averted. For the consequentialist, this attitude is incomprehensible, but for the duty-bound Catholic priest, it is the *only* possible choice. The following anecdote makes this clear: If a parishioner formally confesses that he has planted a bomb in the vestry of a cathedral filled with mourners, the priest is forbidden to act upon the revelation, for the confessional is sacrosanct. From the Church's and the priest's perspective, it is better to allow the building and its inhabitants to be blown up than to nullify the rule and breach confidentiality. This is an extreme case, and this author, notwithstanding his Kantian sympathies, would prefer to save innocent lives despite the abrogation of a normally beneficial rule or duty. What this shows is that some people are deontological consequentialists.

A third possibility is Aristotle's idea that one is ethical when one embraces a virtue (e.g., honesty, generosity), thus confirming moral character. This is known as virtue ethics. It is currently a fairly popular academic modality, but it is improbable that very many people make practical ethical decisions based on or in virtue ethics, especially since Aristotelian philosophy is little known and infrequently applied by the masses in the United States or Europe, let alone in India, China, or Chad. Nevertheless, all of these multitudes are called upon to make ethical decisions concerning helping or harming, feeding or starving, acting with integrity or corrupting through bribes and graft. They do so in accordance with the precepts of their cultures and religions (whether duty or result) and sometimes they purposely make the wrong choices, perhaps because they simply do not care. But when one is hungry, one steals the loaf of bread (and pays the horrific price).

Practical implications for information ethics derive, for some scholars, from the application of ethical thinking: teach the very young to honor others, to act in accordance with suggestions offered by parents and teachers, to never cause harm through the dissemination of false or hurtful information, to not abuse computers, tablets, smart phones, and other digital devices, to not hack or crack or infuse computers or systems with worms or viruses, to not steal or embezzle—to act decently in accordance with the ethical precepts that govern life in the Western world. This is excellent advice; it just happens to be ineffective. Naturally, many computer savvy children grow into young adulthood with an excellent moral compass and go out of their way to do the right thing, but others do not and it only takes a single pathological malcontent to wreak havoc through cracking and exploitation of governmental agencies, utilities, banking organizations, or citizens' personal computers and storage facilities. Sometimes individuals follow the correct path despite general social aberrancy, but they may also be seduced by the prevailing ethos: "Everyone hacks so I will too." In *Moral Man and Immoral Society,* Reinhold Niebuhr posits that individuals act ethically despite general social deviancy.

It is truly astonishing that young men and women decide to dedicate their lives to a career in medicine, with its very difficult path through an onerous education and a subsequently dangerous life filled with the physical bacteria and viruses that visit them every day as well as the psychological torture of dealing with pediatric oncology, among a veritable "tsunami of miseries." There are certainly both monetary and human rewards in an altruistic life dedicated to orthopedic or neurological surgery, but sometimes they are not adequate and doctors and dentists may act despicably. Billions of corrupt dollars are handed over to dishonest medical practitioners. This author recalls the case of a dentist who made a claim, probably to Medicaid, to have done $65,000 worth of fillings in a single day. She was denied; she also went to prison! (See, for example, "Dental Fraud Scams." http://www.insurancefraud.org/scam-alerts-dental.htm)

Ethical considerations have an impact in six major informational areas.

1. *Production* occurs in many venues and takes many forms. Research in the hard and social sciences and the humanities must be accomplished in a fair, considerate, and equitable manner. Human and animal subjects should be treated with respect and compassion. Torture should be abjured. Human subjects should understand the task at hand and the risks of physical or financial harm, privacy incursions, and so on. Informed consent should truly be informed. Chemical and geological work should avoid environmental contamination.

Potential ethical complications defy conception; for example, many concerned people are vehemently against the installation of yet another telescope on Mauna Kea. In social survey and experimental work, it is imperative to fully apprise and debrief participants so that what occurred in the influential but horrifying Tuskegee, Milgram, and Zimbardo experiments is not repeated. Technical and laboratory assistants, post-docs, collaborating contributors (even when there are as many as a thousand), and other ancillary participants should be treated courteously and fairly. Producing excellent and useful research results at the expense of others or the environment is unacceptable and as in Nazi experimental data, should not be disseminated, published, or used. (See next section.) News gathering should be accomplished in an ethically sensitive, nondeceptive manner.

2. *Dissemination* Research results that are not disseminated are otiose. There are many ways in which scholars share their work: Online through email, texts, listservs, and social media; conferences and workshops; publication in hard copy and online journals; the essence of announced or published discoveries in important instances are picked up by the general media. Prior to Arpanet and the Internet, scholars communicated telegraphically, telephonically, but especially postally. This is precisely how Michael Ventris and John Chadwick exchanged data and

information as they struggled to decipher the Linear B puzzle. Only ethically produced, truthful material should be offered to the public, and in an ethically acceptable way.

There is little doubt that the emphasis here is on academic and scientific information dissemination, but the news presented by journalists is equally essential. Early sources were broadsheets posted on buildings or trees, *The Tatler* and *Spectator*, newspapers including *The New York Times*, which continues to appear. A second mode of dissemination developed as radio and then television enhanced their broadcasts. During the 1940s and '50s there were just a few minutes of news available on TV. Today, there exist many full-time news and sports news channels (CNN, MSNBC, ESPN), which cover everything occurring across the globe. Finally, the Internet provides news in many ways, accessible on many devices. With such an avalanche of reports pouring fourth around the world, much that is offered is stilted or false, especially when quoting or allowing a politician such as Donald Trump to speak. He speaks a lot. On October 24, 2016, *The New York Times*, published a two page spread in diminutive type of the hundreds of individuals and organizations that he scorned, demeaned, disparaged, and offended on Twitter, quoting his words over and over again. These "insults and attacks" (Lee) are one of the most astounding and dispiriting things this author has ever seen, vile and repugnant, an unethical abuse of informational communication and at the highest political level. Here are some examples:

- Of Hillary Clinton, who received more than a column and a half: "Crooked, Crooked, Crooked. FAILED ALL OVER THE WORLD, loves to lie"
- Of CNN panelists "a joke, biased, very dumb, Boring, mostly losers in life!"
- Of *Forbes* magazine: "failed magazine, circulation way down, failing, failing"
- Of John McCain: "Very foul mouthed, has done nothing ... incapable of dong anything ... graduated last in his class ... dummy"
- Of Mexico: "totally corrupt, we get the killers, drugs and crime ... they get the money!" (Lee).

Even an important newspaper such as *Pravda* (ironically, "truth") is notorious for falsification and a well-respected paper such as *The Wall Street Journal* is so agenda-driven that some of what it publishes is prejudicial rather than objective reporting. Yellow journalism is not just the dead step-child of William Hearst. The "melodrama, romance, and hyperbole" he foisted on the public can still be found in many venues including conservative talk radio and supermarket tabloids such as the *Globe,* whose covers proclaim "Croc Hunter Committed Suicide" (November 16, 2016) or "Charles Seizes Throne in Palace Coup" (November 21, 2016). And journalists also make some very costly mistakes; informational abuse can have dire consequences: Gawker's bankruptcy can be traced directly to its publication of the Hulk Hogan sex tape and *Rolling Stone* lost a defamation suit for unfairly blaming an academic dean for malfeasance, when a purported gang rape occurred at the University of Virginia; the entire business was based on a witness's fraudulent accusation (Sisario B1).

Even worse, of course, are the news stories fabricated by a group of foolish and naive journalists including Stephen Glass, Jayson Blair, and Janet Cooke, who apparently thought they would not be caught. (See Robillard for an anthology of journalistic fabulists.) A more sinister aspect of dissemination concerns *WikiLeaks* revelations, which are discussed below. It must be noted in passing that these anomalous dissemblers as well as those who propagate fake news should not deter us from recalling that journalists usually provide excellent and truthful coverage of what is occurring in the often dangerous world and may be hounded, harassed, imprisoned, and murdered for their efforts.

3. *Storage* modalities have altered over the centuries: clay tablets, monumental inscriptions, papyrus scrolls, various natural materials such as bark and leaves, quipu, parchment scrolls and manuscripts, books, and countless electronic media such as wax, vinyl, tape, floppy disk, CD, and online facilities and clouds. It is a never-ending task to keep up with these changes. No matter what advantages the most recent avatar offers, the printed book (and periodical), which has served us for almost 600 years, is the most permanent, easily accessible, and convenient means of conveying information. It is foolish to store data and information knowing that the device will soon fail resulting in complete loss. (See Chapter 9.)

4. *Access* to scholarly information requires a purchase, subscription,

trip to a facility, or an organization willing to mail documents to one's home; for Internet access, one must have a device capable of connecting to it and permission to do so by making a monthly payment. For non–hard copy materials in collections, one must have the appropriate reader or scanner, otherwise even microform images are often impossible to see. Digital materials are unreadable without the sometimes dated, broken, stored, or missing hardware. For middle class people, not having convenient access to the Internet is inconceivable. For those who live in poverty—the homeless, those without enough money to purchase food or medicines—access is a luxury. Some of these people may have cell phones, but a non-accessing TracFone purchased for an initial payment of $15 and with an $80 annual subscription fee is quite different from an iPhone 7 at $700 with an annual cost of more than a $1,000, a burden to many. In Third World countries, there exist hard working, industrious people who earn a dollar a day; that is less than $400 a year; $1,000 a year is not atypical in the poorer lands. In any case, Internet access is out of the question at all, because although one might encounter a snow leopard or gorilla, there are few if any libraries, schools, or Internet cafes in rural areas of Nepal or the Central African Republic. Access to life-enhancing information is unavailable to about two thirds of the world's population. This is an ethical debacle. (See Chapter 9.)

5. *Search and Retrieval* Not long ago, enormous companies, like the now defunct FIND/SVP (with its 3,000 employees), earned large sums of money ($175,000,000) locating data and information for commercial clients, some of whom kept these companies on retainer. Subsequently, even libraries began to offer fee-based services. Reference librarians in public, academic, and special facilities helped and guided patrons to and through complex searches. Specialized medical, legal, and business information professionals still help, but the advent and swift development of a free, replete, and fairly comprehensive informational data base (the Internet) and many sophisticated search engines, most made obsolete by Google, have replaced much dependent searching in hard copy indices or online. Now even a novice can quickly locate an astonishingly high percentage of what he or she is seeking. That it requires incisive acumen, critical thinking, to assess the validity and value of the material is another matter; this is a skill that evolves over a lifetime. Lamentably many people

never learn how to differentiate the distorted trash from the useful information. Some do not really care.

6. *Use, Application, Misuse*

For too long, the scientific community held the position that researchers sought solutions to problems; their goal was to discover knowledge (in order to predict and control). Applications were best left to technologists. What is of vital importance here is that scientists refused to admit that they should take responsibility for the results of their discoveries. Things have changed. The misuse of information garnered from unethical production methods is perfectly exemplified in the ironically practicable results of Nazi atrocities. In the *Pernkopf Atlas* case, the eponymous author dissected the bodies of murdered victims from which he created a magnificent anatomical atlas, a "tainted beauty." It is still used today in medical work, but some practitioners question whether it should be consulted at all (Israel, Howard passim). The same is true of the Nazi climate experiments that yielded excellent data but at the expense of suffering human beings. If one were to place ethical mandates at the head of a ranked list of reasons to abjure usage, all the research results of Nazi heinousness would be obliterated, because ends do not justify means. Nevertheless, when other considerations are taken into account, many of the affected affirm application.

Law

Obviously, with few strictures, ineffective moral suasion, and little impetus to act correctly, when deviating often brings extraordinary rewards (think of Bernard Madoff and his enormous scam, once thought to hover at 65 billion dollars but now reduced to a mere 20 billion), the empowered turn to legal means of controlling the wayward. When ethics fails, the law intervenes, and the law in capitalist societies, especially the United States, favors property over human considerations. Kill a cat burglar in defense of one's family and one *may* be prosecuted for manslaughter or in some circumstances even second degree murder, but steal money and one will end up with a 150 year sentence. The strange thing is that the Internet provides viewers with countless ways to wreak havoc, but no government agency intervenes: terrorism, hacking and cracking, the sale of stolen credit card numbers, child pornography, trolling, and many other horrible illegal activities are all monitored, tolerated, and flourish, and not necessarily in deference to First Amendment free speech protection, a concept that does not exist in many other countries, where governments could take action but do not. The law is clear and if such activities occurred anywhere other than in cyberspace, they would be shut down and the perpetrators punished. That billions of dollars are lost to Internet scams is not widely advertised; that government agencies and the military are constantly hacked speaks badly for cyberspace security. The failure of the law to locate and punish is breathtaking, and sometimes not *only* in cyberspace: Fraud involving credit cards, scams, welfare, medicine, as well as tax evasion cost Americans extraordinary amounts of money.

Just as ethics attempts to control aberrant behavior but often fails, so too does the law (by its very existence) often attempt but fail in this often impossible task, but the difference is that the law has a true coercive force to back it up. Ethical failure results in the triumph of evil; legal failure can at least lead to control through fines and imprisonment. Here is how this works: When a person abrogates his loyalty to his country, especially when allegiance is sworn in the military, and additionally in a position in which classified materials are involved, ethical commitment has obviously failed. The law impinges, the person is arrested, tried, convicted, and sentenced to a long prison term. So it was with Bradley (now Chelsea) Manning and Edward Snowdon too, at least hypothetically, since he escaped to Russia.

Some well-meaning people confuse these traitors' actions with whistleblowing, which entails *indicating* that someone or some entity is acting unethically or illegally. It does not give the whistleblower the right to fail in his own duties and to indiscriminately release troves of material that is none of the public's or the enemy's business and that may cause harm and death to others. The claim that the documents were revelatory is only partially correct. Even minimally knowledgeable citizens are aware of the many secretive agencies (NSA, FBI, CIA and even the Stasi* and

---

*The East German Stasi kept vials of its citizens' body odors on file so that they could be traced and identified if they tried to escape to the West.

KGB from now defunct countries) that monitor and surveil everyone and everything. Additionally, non-governmental surveillance cameras riddle the streets of most big cities, especially London and New York, and even diminutive towns in bucolic Vermont have these cameras affixed to street light stanchions in order to track traffic malefactors and earn vast sums of money, which is divided between the town and the private company that monitors them.

The empowered know everything: Privacy is dead and one should get over it, as the cynic noted. But he is wrong. And do these same defenders speak up for other cyber-thieves and traitors? Contractor Harold T. Martin III's lawyers tell us that he "has devoted his entire career to serving his country"—by stealing "500 million pages of government documents" among which is top-secret material, some of which he stored in his car. He "betray[ed] the trust of the nation" (Shane). Should he too be praised as a whistleblower?

Readers should not misapprehend the aim here. Action based on good intention, that is, ethical commitment and a caring, socially acceptable attitude, is always preferable to legal mandates and machinations, some of which are obscenely misguided and harmful, based as they are on poorly adjudicated cases that act as precedent and statutes passed by self-serving legislators who favor themselves and their wealthy supporters. One merely has to recall laws that protected plantation owners at the expense of their slaves, anti-miscegenation legislation, or Nazi mandates that made possible the purifying annihilation of many millions of people, including, incredibly, disabled World War I German veterans and Jehovah's Witnesses. The law is a harsh mistress; it demands and requires conformity, but also disobedience when truly warranted, as Thoreau, Gandhi, and Martin Luther King have so tellingly shown.

What is truly inconceivable is the dichotomous nature of the concept of ethics and the law in relation to certain actions. For example, falsification, fabrication, or plagiary in scientific research and especially in clinical trials can have a devastating, even fatal effect on human beings. These actions are highly unethical and would be condemned by everyone including peers, and so one might expect that the law would demand retribution, but even when the work is funded by the federal government, the law may not fully control and punish the perpetrator. When unfunded,

2. Ethics and Law

there is no one except a district attorney or the justice department to prosecute, but they are apparently too busy with embezzlers and whistle-blowers. Guilty researchers and academics will probably not lose their positions. Ethically, there is a horrific failure here. Legally, not much occurs.

3   Theory

"...[Derek] Parfit ... explored issues in moral choice that reanimated the field of ethics, which had descended into abstruse technical analyses of moral terms like 'ought,' 'good' and 'right.'"—William Grimes

Floridi and Capurro are theoreticians. Capurro's later philosophical structuring seems to contradict what he offers in "Towards an Ontological Foundation of Information Ethics," in which he returns to ancient Greece in order to adduce truth-telling and especially in relation to intercultural information ethics, wherein harmony, respect, and courtesy are controlling factors. This long Western tradition of IE is characterized by freedom of speech and print, to which is now added freedom of access. These introductory remarks are followed by a discussion of Heideggerian metaphysics in order to advocate for "Digital ontology ... [as] today's pervading casting of Being." Even if Capurro is correct that digital being is "our *Zeitgeist*," which is unlikely (just because many people in some parts of the world are electronically interconnected and walk around staring at smart phones, does not mean that humans are digital beings), I am not sure that an ontological foundation of IE based on a "digital casting of being" and "locat[ing] it within a phenomenological interpretation of human existence..." is truly beneficial. And this leads to "The ethical question asked by information ethics, ... 'What is good for our bodily being-in-the-world with others in particular?'" It is extremely difficult to see the actual, the practical, the necessary connection between these philosophical remarks and the few practical problems noted at the conclusion of his extremely long and complex paper, one that cites Aquinas, Aristotle, Foucault, Floridi, Heidegger, Kant, Popper, Wittgenstein, and countless other sometimes incomprehensible thinkers (Capurro, "Towards" passim).

---

3. Theory

In 2013, Floridi published *The Ethics of Information*, his most relevant study but his inverted title is not quite the same thing as "information ethics," in the same way that, as a scholar observed, a horse chestnut is not a chestnut horse. He does, however, switch to information ethics as he proceeds through the book. It is certainly strange that of the present author's hundreds of germane books, articles, papers, columns, editorials, reviews, and letters, Floridi cites just *Ethical Challenges in Librarianship*, the 1988 volume in which IE is merely noted, as well as a collection he coedited. All the rest is ignored. Even the prolific Capurro appears only once. The bibliography, however, contains citations to 49 of Floridi's studies.

This citational curiosity is easily explained by the fact that the practical work that most scholars have done in the field during the past 40 years does not jibe with his philosophical and theoretical conceptualization of IE, which he defines in a complex hierarchy of stages, whereas it has traditionally merely been a subdiscipline of normative ethics that deals with the production, dissemination, access, storage, retrieval, and application of data, information, and knowledge. Floridi admits as much but uses very different terminology, and is more concerned with IE as an environmental ethics and "The global infosphere, or how information is becoming our ecosystem" (3, 21, 8).

Floridi lays out a series of stages in IE's evolution: first "as an ethics of informational resources" (reliability, quality) (21), second, of products (liability, plagiary) (23), third, of the environment (privacy) (24), and fourth as a macroethics (combining all three) (25–26). But the present author finds this rather disingenuous. From the outset, IE has assumed under its rubric all of these modalities and many others. And Floridi wants to move away from a purely epistemological deployment of information to one that also includes an ontological perspective (28), despite the fact that information is a *known* entity not a reality unto itself.

Although traditional issues (privacy, viruses, information warfare, etc.) are certainly inherent here, Floridi indicates that he will not discuss them (1). Instead he is interested in a "constructionist philosophy" to explain "semantic artefacts" (2). This, because we find ourselves in a "hyperhistorical predicament" (3). Well, Floridi is a philosopher who favors complexity and a great deal of esoteric terminology. And so this secondary strain of IE is confusing and perhaps not all that helpful. Floridi spends some time explaining levels of abstraction. Despite the present author's diverse studies of philosophy as an undergraduate and graduate student (at several American and foreign institutions), he does not understand the concept, its necessity, nor its applicability to IE: "...the development of information ethics as a macroethics requires a change in our view of the world, in our ontological perspective" (29). And so here, with an additional neologism, is how informational privacy is attacked: "Once telepistemics is understood as a way of making the observed locally present ... a privacy breach is more easily comparable to a case of metaphorical abduction..." (50). Does all of this seem reasonable? Is it helpful in any way in explaining and solving privacy incursions? Even more mystifying are his "four ethical principles of IE,"

> 0 entropy ought not to be caused in the infosphere (null law)
> 1 entropy ought to be prevented in the infosphere
> 2 entropy ought to be removed from the infosphere
> 3 the flourishing of informational entities as well as of the whole infosphere ought to be promoted by preserving, cultivating, and enriching their well-being [71]

and the many often terminologically obtuse statements he relishes: Information ethics is "a development of environmental ethics" (133); "an ecopoietic ethics requires a *philosophy of information* that can ground an *informational anthropology*" (168); "Informational privacy ... [is] a function of ontological friction" (231). This bombardment of disparate, often bizarre, terminology is quite confusing, disconcerting, and irritating.

Capurro disagrees with Floridi and here follows a long extract from a preliminary remark that Capurro offers to a detailed critique of Floridi:

> In his paper "A defense of information structural realism" [*Synthese* 2009, Vol. 61, No. 2, pp. 219–253] Floridi argues that digital ontology deals with the view that "the ultimate nature of reality is digital." This is, indeed, as Floridi stresses, an uncritical pre-kantian view. But what Floridi calls "digital ontology" is in fact digital metaphysics. Using the term "ontology" with regard to his own theory, namely "informational ontology" ("the ultimate nature of reality is structural"), Floridi is no less metaphysical or pre-kantian and his argument is self-contradictory.
>
> When I talk about digital ontology I am taking no position with regard to the digital as "the ultimate nature of reality." I am just saying that in the present age, the digital seems to be (at least it seems to me) the prevalent perspective for understanding (!) beings in their being. This is an epistemological (in

3. Theory

Heideggerian terms: an "ontological") view, not a metaphysical (or "ontological" in Floridi's terms) one. But, indeed, this ontological perspective can become a metaphysical one. Floridi denies the legitimacy of such a digital Pythagoreism, and I agree with him in this point. But he makes the case for a kind of informational Platonism which is no less metaphysical than the digital one he criticizes. Floridi's "infosphere" is nothing but a Platonic phantasy [Capurro "On"].

There is nothing wrong with philosophical conjecturing, but Floridi has turned a practical normative branch of ethics into a convoluted conundrum, and there is so much overemphasis on and confusion of a terminology that under normal circumstances is clearly demarcated, that it leaves one reeling:

1. It is extremely improbable that most people or even philosophically-minded scholars would sympathize with the presumption that "the ultimate nature of reality is digital." This is reminiscent of earlier misguided theories that equated reality with whatever was popular at the time, for example, reality is a mechanism, like a clock.

2. Capurro claims that Floridi's digital ontology is actually digital metaphysics. Since ontology is one of the two branches of metaphysics (the other is cosmology), this makes even less sense than the phrase itself.

3. Metaphysics deals with the nature of reality, epistemology with knowledge: how one knows and how one knows what one knows is true. This transition from ontology/metaphysics to epistemology is incomprehensible.

4. Capurro indicates that Floridi's "infosphere" is a "Platonic fantasy."

Well, Platonic ideational reality is metaphorically comprehensible, though highly improbable. What is less useful in the practical world that information ethics serves is an "infosphere" and its concomitant baggage.

It is unpleasant and painful to criticize the thought of respected colleagues,* but the insertion of a host of inappropriate terms (information ecology, for example) is strikingly reminiscent of the misapplication of scientific terminology and concepts (entropy, Heisenberg's Uncertainty

---

*Not all people, scholars, and academics are so caring and thoughtful. Indeed, academics are infamous for their bitter and nasty altercations within departments and across disciplines. Some of these folks are vile and cause real mental, emotional, and professional harm to colleagues. In a grotesque case, perpetrated precisely by those people who one might expect to *think* before acting, an unknown though suspected person mailed excrement to four university professors of philosophy, all of whom happen to be defenders of women and minorities' rights in the discipline of philosophy. Here, ethical information dissemination is replaced by excremental communication (Schuessler).

Principle, Schrödinger's cat, the big bang and quantum theories, and time) in literary works and the misappropriation of these same ideas, concepts, or principles in postmodernist critical thought, where the authors misunderstand, misconstrue, and embarrass themselves, what Alan Sokal refers to as fashionable nonsense. In an incisive comment, Bielby confirms the misdirection that IE seems to have taken where "a unified taxonomy for the field of Information Ethics" appears to be impossible:

> Perhaps for many, the evolution of the field of Information Ethics from its inception (either in 1948 or the 1980s, depending on one's perspective) to its current state feasibly paints a sort of runaway scene, whereby the application of ethical praxis to the real life concerns of information and communications technology have all but been hijacked and subsumed into grander philosophical deliberations about the nature of reality and being. Where once the literature and scholarship of the field addressed head-on the concerns of intellectual property, privacy, freedom of access and social responsibility (concerns that most people could follow and understand), the present state of Information Ethics seems conceivably elitist, fallen prey perhaps to ivory tower scholasticism. The debate, some might surmise, has escaped the house and is no longer accessible by those to whom it concerns, and is now, as worded by Charles Ess, a "difficult debate between Floridi's Philosophy of Information as a philosophical naturalism and the Heideggarian components of Rafael Capurro's intercultural information ethics" [Ess, 2009]. And so, to the uninitiated eye, where once Information Ethics boasted a call to action, it has betrayed the pursuit of worldly good in favor of a sort of cosmic ontological reconciliation of informational entities. And while this grand standing works wonders for philosophers, the average worker might wonder if there is any room left for action on the part of the rest of us [Bielby, II].

It may help to try to understand what a theory entails. Most people consider theories to be, well, theoretical—academic, with no realistic applicability. But this is not accurate. A theory is merely an explanation and influential theories abound: heliocentrism, evolution, relativity, plate tectonics, but also some less probable choices. Shannon's Information theory and Alistair Duff's "Normative Theory of the Information Society" already exist; it is certainly possible that a theory of information *ethics* could have some applicability, but it is generally superfluous* in the

---

*An example of an apparently helpful and palliating practice, according to those who avail themselves of it, undergirded by a bizarre and evidence-free theoretical foundation, is chiropractic. The human anatomy and physiology that practitioners study is valid; subluxation theory, however, probably has little connection to reality, and some chiropractors dismiss it.

hazardous informational world that humans now inhabit: It is wrong to steal data. If people cannot ethically control their kleptomaniacal urges, then the law's guardians should pay them a visit. A theory of data theft does very little for the victims.

The most telling indictment is Tony Doyle's deconstruction of Floridian IE. Doyle indicates "that the moral community should [**not**] be expanded," that is, not everything deserves informational valuation; he points out flaws in Floridi's critique of consequentialism; and he notes a lacuna of practical implications. There is much more detail in this excellent paper (Doyle, "Critique" passim).

There is a bottom line and it is that IE has evolved in two strains, the first initiated within librarianship where the unquestioned provision of information pitted arbitrary (and potentially damaging) professional demands against ethical social commitment, among many other pressing matters long ignored or stifled in a sea of coded mandates.

Simultaneously, and then later, an emphasis on less practical philosophizing and bizarre theoretical posturing resulted in the kind of work that Capurro and Floridi favor at least in their own studies. Naturally, Capurro, as the editor of *IRIE*, accepts diverse material including practical studies for publication. Floridi's "information ethics" is not the present author's information ethics; it does not reflect the work that he and others have done during the past 40 years, ever since the 1976 publication of "Professionalism or Culpability? An Experiment in Ethics" (Hauptman).

Ethics is a practical branch of philosophy, implemented in order to ensure correct action. A theoretical framework or foundation is both necessary and superfluous, necessary for structuration and legitimation but superfluous for the practical implementation of ethical decision-making in informational pursuits. Consider an analogy: biology is undergirded by various theoretical structures. The present author once asked his mother, who taught regents molecular biology, how much time she allocated to Darwin and evolutionary theory. The answer was none. The regents test did not contain any questions on evolution. It was not interested in taxonomy or morphology, natural history or species differentiation or identification; it cared about anatomy and physiological processes such as respiration, the Krebs cycle, and hormonal or genetic influences. Theory could wait until college or graduate school!

The Scope of Information Ethics

Here is a critique followed by some speculative thought, but of a more practical and perhaps practicable nature than Floridi's or Capurro's theorizing. Floridi's appropriation of information ethics and his extreme philosophical position have resulted in a general misunderstanding, one that Richard Volkman undertakes to correct—except, of course, that he has no idea what IE actually entails and is more interested in rescuing virtue ethics from oblivion. It is sad indeed that Volkman (and perhaps others) misconstrue, misinterpret, and misunderstand and now think that Floridian and therefore traditional IE is an addition to or substitute for deontological or consequentialist modes of ethical decision-making. It is not. Rather, IE is a subset of practical ethics that deals with informational problems that the application of rules or the consideration of potential consequences can often solve.

Information Ethics is not an ethical modality nor system; rather, it is a rubric that encompasses traditional informational entities and this does *not* include everything in the universe (which reflects Floridi's "ontological equality"), since every stone, every cow, and every galaxy are not informational entities worthy of *informational* respect and coddling. It would be much better to respect the cow as a living, sentient organism and not slaughter it than to claim that it is informational in nature and that all information at all times and in all places must be retained. As Volkman (lamentably) observes, "...the great historical contribution of [Floridian] IE, will be to reveal once and for all the absurdity of extending impartiality and universality where they do not belong" (383). Additionally, human beings are not merely informational nor digital organisms. But it also must be noted that Volkman's virtue ethics with its "antifoundationalist, particularist, and relativist" (380) agenda is hardly an improvement on Floridi's perspective.

On the other hand, Alistair Duff presents a complex normative theory of the information society, one that derives from his contention that there exists a confused state of affairs concerning the social norms shaping technological change ("Normative" 3), the result of which is a "moral labyrinth" (4). He postulates a social ethics of information that will bring about "political and legal action" and an "ethical information policy" (6) in order to minimize the commodification of information (17). For Duff, information is characterized by "referentiality and truth" rather than practical matters

(23) and falsity is excluded from the informational world that he is postulating (25). The goal, naturally, is a just society (54). And, therefore, information, contrary to the present author's position (see Chapter 13), is seen as a basic right (59). Here is "a prescriptive formula for the social distribution of information" (63) in order to bring about social equity (95).

The concluding and most difficult part of Duff's program is his suggestion that a solution can be found in social engineering (99), something that even many liberals will find hard to digest. But whatever means is formulated and accepted, the goal must be an ethical attitude toward and application of information in a just and caring world.

Finally, in "What Is Information Ethics?" Kay Mathiesen proposes a prolegomenon to or a framework for a theory of IE. The key components, naturally, are information, understood in a diverse but not overly broad nor purely technical sense, and ethics. In contradistinction to Shannon, Floridi, and others, her theory has immediate practicable value. Information must be abstract and have syntactic and semantic value; it must be comprehensible and presumably accurate; the relationship between information and people must be specified. The value of the information access state, which may be understood in terms of rights, should be emphasized. The key point is that "...the focus of an information ethic should be on the value that access states have for human beings." This is practicably applicable to the many issues presented in this study.

Negation of Ethics

I have never encountered the position that Bruce Waller advances in *Against Moral Responsibility* and which he indicates is part and parcel of the Western intellectual tradition (by citing various scholarly advocates unknown to me). It is perhaps the most bizarre serious (non)ethical position one might consider: It claims that moral responsibility is irrelevant and harmful. Moral accountability, which Waller indicates has to do with "giving an account" rather than being accountable, that is, responsible for one's actions, is a red herring here: We either have free will or do not but are never morally responsible for the good or evil we perpetrate. For Waller, punishment and reward are counterproductive.

His position would be more comprehensible if he were a determinist (and one author claims that he is); it is extremely difficult to understand how he reconciles his free will ("Free will is not a philosophical construct, but a basic power of animals like ourselves for whom open options are advantageous..."; "Moral responsibility abolitionism does not reject free choices...") with the absolute genetic inheritance and environmental influence that control his evildoers, who are therefore not morally responsible for their heinous crimes and so do not deserve punishment, which he thinks is limited to barbaric vindictiveness; but sometimes people do deserve to be punished and/or incarcerated.

"It is obvious that we do not make ourselves: ultimately, we are the products of an elaborate evolutionary, genetic, cultural, and conditioning history." Thus, to invert Sartre, "Essence precedes existence." Nevertheless, we do make choices but are not morally responsible for the outcome primarily because it would be *unfair*. This is Waller's consistent and repeated mantra. It is specious and false to indicate that genetic and environmental influences determine one's destiny,

If every professional philosopher (and let us throw in all theoretical psychologists as well) agreed that Waller is correct, the man and woman in the street (or the pasture) would go right on exercising their will, holding others morally responsible, ascribing blame, and demanding justice. This is what appears to be *fair* to them.

4 Research

Although research is perhaps the most abused term in the academic lexicon, it is, nevertheless, the foundation upon which innovation, invention, and progress stand. It begins in grammar school where children barely able to read are sent on a quest to research various topics. Seventy years ago, when the present author was perhaps seven and in the second grade, he wrote a paper on crustaceans, which he typed! He knows because he still has it. It is so substantively accurate and so mellifluously articulated that no child could produce it; he apparently simply copied it from an encyclopedia. Not only was he not criticized; the paper was complimented. Here, instituting the research process was counter-productive, since all he learned to do was plagiarize. Once he was old enough to understand what was expected of him, he never did that again, though he continued research through high school, college,and eleven years of graduate study.

Sometimes contemporary high school students, who know virtually nothing about a topic, let alone a discipline (history, literary criticism, astronomy) and its conventions, are admonished not only to do a major research project but also to locate primary documents, a task that is now, at least in essence, more easily accomplished than it was before archivists began posting facsimiles of original texts on the Internet. Viewing materials online is not the same as handling them in a special collection, but it will do for a high school freshman in rural Nebraska. Indeed, the point here is that until one has a decent command of a discipline, research is unnecessary and requiring the accessing of primary materials is foolish. If one cannot differentiate between Louis XIV and Jean-Paul Marat or Enrico Fermi and Albert Einstein, reading (and handling) their holographic correspondence, though potentially exciting, is not a useful exercise.

Historical, archeological, literary, or sociological research, for example, is warranted and will often produce useful and practicable outcomes, but searching in archives, middens, memoirs, or urban playgrounds is not the same thing as experimenting in a chemical or biological laboratory. It is here in controlled experiments that the term has true applicability. The scientist investigates a meaningful hypothesis, following a strict protocol, discovers something earth shattering and informs the world, preferably through an article in *Science* or *Nature*. Things go well and he (or she) wins the Nobel Prize.

The problem is that the conclusions are wrong. John Ioannidis claims that a very high percentage of research results, especially in biomedicine, are false. There are many reasons for this (statistical inaccuracy, misaligned instrumentation, inadvertent error, manipulation, misconduct), and when the results cannot be replicated, the paper may be retracted. Accidentally misinforming peers and the public is regrettable and embarrassing for the well-meaning scientist; it may have a deleterious effect on one's career, but in reality, it is easily forgivable, though one might hope that in the future he or she will be more meticulous. When the substantive content or even just the conclusions of a paper have been purposely distorted in some way, the miscreant should be severely punished, though often he or she gets off with a mild reprimand.

Research in all fields but especially in science may have detrimental results. It is for this reason, rather than theological or governmental strictures, that the contemporary notion of forbidden knowledge has been postulated. In 1996, Roger Shattuck explored the concept in a book length work; three years later Deborah Johnson observed that since science may not actually aim for objective truth, traditional "freedom of inquiry" should perhaps be delimited. Decisions concerning limitations should be "made from a position of ... partial knowledge," since humans are not omniscient, and scientists must accept that knowledge is not disinterested; that is, it has a stake. The bottom line is that "Much more attention should be focused on choosing directions in science, and as this is done, the matter of whether constraints should be placed on science will fall into place" ("Reframing" abstract).

Institutional Review Boards

Academics tend to forget or ignore the fact that corporate and non-profit laboratories as well as independent scholars do a great deal of invaluable research. These people are not compelled to have an institutional review board (IRB) examine, analyze, evaluate, and vet any proposed research that involves human beings or animals. But academics, hospitals, and federally funded work must, and without approval they may not proceed with impunity. There is little doubt that researchers cause harm and therefore the concept of an IRB is beneficial, but like peer review it causes a great deal of unwarranted misery. The IRB members may be ill-equipped to understand the esoteric disciplinary material, misunderstand matters, or hold up or stifle the proposed work. Such review boards should be rethought; some people think they should be eliminated. In a brief column, Richard Shweder and Richard Nisbett argue that research should be deregulated. And the government is interested in exempting from IRB review research that does not pose a real threat and this is an excellent development according to these authors. But their position is too extreme and humans and animals will suffer even more than they do, if this were to occur. (See Cohen for an extended discussion.)

The Internet

In the early days of cyberspace access, this author claimed that there is really no difference between ethical action in the real world and what should now occur in the digital realm. The same attitudes, modalities, norms, rules, and laws that obtain here are also operative wherever the Internet might lead. He still holds that this is the case. Then one might well wonder why Internet research ethics (IRE) has become a distinct and burgeoning category. Accessing materials in special collections or archives requires honesty and care, courtesy and adherence to the particular rules that govern the institution, whose mandate might be to serve the scholarly public but which does not have to share its materials with those who manifest a threat of some kind. The Morgan Library and Museum, for example, requires scholars to contact it beforehand and indicate why a visit to its non-public areas is necessary. Online access demands the same attentiveness.

In the case of survey research, IRB approval, informed consent, consideration, and data sharing should take place regardless of location.

But there are some major differences and that is why IRE has received specific attention. Indeed, there is such extensive interest here that the Association of Internet Researchers (http://aoir.org/ethics/) offers some precise suggestions in "Ethical decision-making and Internet research 2.0: Recommendations from the AoIR ethics working committee," a 2012 report: Protect the vulnerable and human subjects generally, consider the rights of subjects versus the research results as well as harms and risks. There is much more in this very detailed document. (See also Elizabeth Buchanan's edited volume, *Readings in Virtual Research Ethics*.)

Scientific misconduct's three major transgressions—falsification, fabrication, and plagiarism—as well as a multitude of other ethical breaches including cooking and trimming data, uninformed consent, and financial conflicts of interest, can occur in any discipline or area. Some of the sciences (biomedicine) and the social sciences (psychology) are more prone to ethical malfeasance than humanistic disciplines (philosophy, musicology) but no area is immune to the perils presented by an ethically demanding world. The following chapters discuss these matters.

Documentation and Authorial Ethics

Documentation

There exist two related topics, documentation and authorial ethics, both of which this author has covered in monographic studies. It is obvious that the latter subject is precisely pertinent here but it may come as a shock that the simple act of documenting would have relevance in or to information ethics. As it happens, documentation and its attendant miseries are not as simple as the typical researcher might think. Indeed, for most writers (from kindergarteners to Nobelists), documentation is merely a reference to a source included in a foot- or end- note, reference list, or bibliography, the construction of which used to be an onerous task for those more intent on their narratives or texts. This is no longer the case because the citation is now sometimes provided in the source or software can do the work for the inept and in any one of hundreds of systems from

4. Research

APA (psychology) and MLA (literature) to the Blue- or Maroon-books (law) and Chicago (many publishers).* But there is much more to documentation and here it will suffice to concisely mention areas in which unethical activity all too frequently occurs.

Within citational listings, one finds errors, ghosts, padding, inappropriate material, and references to journal editors' and their publications' works cajoled (bullied) from the author. Any form of misleading data impedes the reader who wishes to follow up on sources. The error rate in citations is truly astonishing. In scientific citation systems, first names are limited to initials; in the citation indices, there may be a Tom Jones, a Tim Jones, and a Tod Jones; they are all noted as T. Jones. Is this helpful?

Publishers elide, shift, transfer, or eliminate notes and bibliographies in order to save money. Sometimes the documentation for a monograph (or even a journal article) is available only on a website, where it, like their texts, can be altered or expunged. Substantive notes, which are nonexistent in some disciplines but very frequent in others, may be misleading, inappropriate, or self-serving. In law reviews (bizarrely, edited by law school students), notes are abused to such a degree that many jurists (Abner Mikva, for example) abjure them entirely, that is, they neither read, consult, nor write them.

In some venues, biblical studies, for example, notes contain remarks and critiques, some of which stretch back 1,000 years. Rashi's† commentary on the Torah is included side by side with scripture and when studying often supplants the actual text, physically on the page and intellectually, when people are learning, that is, studying. It may at times be as difficult for a seriously committed scholar to disagree with Rashi as it would be to question the validity of the sacred text. Depending on many factors, the

---

*This author constructs his own citations as he creates the text (in APA or MLA depending on what he is doing) and benefits dramatically: he enjoys the process; he memorizes the data and then can recall it (years) later; he maintains an immediate and direct connection between the text and the bibliography so that citations are not mislaid, elided, confused, or lost. In the future, a reviewer will not be able to accuse him of plagiary and he will not have to lay the blame on his *hundreds of assistants* who did *not* write his review, paper, or book (of which there are approximately 700 items).

†Rashi is an acronym for Rabbi Solomon ben Isaac, who lived in the 11th century. It is easier to see this if one contracts his Hebrew name: Rabbi Shlomo ben Yitzak. Another famous example is the Rambam (Rabbi Moses ben Maimon—Maimonides).

same thing may be said of biblical commentators such as the Venerable Bede and Thomas Aquinas and analogous works on Buddhist scripture pored over by monks and nuns in lamaseries in Nepal and other countries.

Illustrative images are a form of documentation and they too can present many ethical problems. In some instances the image (table, figure, map, drawing, print, painting, radiograph, or photograph) alters the material and may be more important than the textual discussion. A study of lesser known art, or architectural or photographic works, require images to make the discussion comprehensible; their absence is an ethical breach and this occurs quite often. (Now it is possible to refer a reader to a website where the images are made available, a rather ineffective solution to a publisher's ineptitude or greed.) The images may supplant or contradict the text and they can be misleading or patently false. This is discussed in more detail in Chapter 19.

Authorial Ethics

Many ethical infractions can occur in the authorial environment, which is not limited exclusively to those who create texts but also involves various types of editors, publishers, and sometimes even printers and distributors. But it should be obvious that authors are of prime importance here, for they often do very unsavory things. They purposely falsify, fabricate, and plagiarize (see Chapters 5 and 6); scholars produce ostensibly valid results that Ioannidis claims are very frequently false; they are careless and introduce meaningful errors into their work; they purposely or inadvertently misinform and confuse; ideologues with extreme (and often false) agenda of any persuasion indoctrinate in such a way that many sometimes-gullible people (who lack true critical abilities and acumen) accept and believe what is handed to them by preachers, politicians, think tank propagandists, hoaxers, and the creators of fake news, which has become a ubiquitous problem especially on social media (much of what one knows derives from authority and questioning it is an essential aspect of the thoughtful person); they can be corrupt, have conflicts of interest, and may not care much about informed consent or the protection of research subjects.

4. Research

Perhaps the outstanding example of unethical experimental activity (other than the Holocaust) is the deception that psychologists have perpetrated in the past but continue to defend in the present. Stanley Milgram's "shocking" experiment is the locus classicus, but he was preceded by many others and scholars continue to follow in his footsteps. For example, William Epstein is notorious for his deceptive experimental forays, through which he does show, for example, that confirmational bias exists but at the expense of those he deceives. And scholarly deception sometimes becomes part of the knowledge base and it is very difficult to expunge.

Richard Hamilton provides evidence that Max Weber, in *The Protestant Ethic and the Spirit of Capitalism,* and Michel Foucault, in *Discipline and Punish,* were both guilty of blatant deception in the claims that they advanced. The former's footnotes are misleading or inaccurate (42, 43), among other problems, and the latter ignores prison reform and progress and indicates that Bentham's Panopticon was extremely influential but does not inform the reader that it was not actually built (175). Many additional problems exist with Foucault's work but adherents and defenders do not care, evidence is ignored, and myths continue to misinform. This is the case with many other works in which authors purposely deceive. It is perhaps most prevalent in life-writing: biography but especially autobiography and memoir, where it may be difficult or impossible to root out mendacity; and those who distort the truth tell us that it is okay to do so.

5 Science

The hard sciences follow a very precise protocol, which has come to be called the scientific method. It is especially appropriate when dealing with inanimate often easily controllable entities; it is less successful, for example, in clinical trials where humans fail to cooperate, prevaricate, or die. The method used in the laboratory, the clinic, and the natural astronomical and terrestrial worlds is:

- empirical
- objective
- experimental or observational
- randomizing
- (doubly) blinding
- controlling of all variables
- systematic
- cumulative
- verifiable and replicable.

Naturally, it is easier to maintain absolute control in a physics laboratory than in a clinical trial. Thus, there is a ranked progression of control from chemistry at the apex, through physics, and astronomy, to the least successful sciences, so far, biology and geology. Eventually, if things continue as they have since the Enlightenment, all of the sciences will reach a point where near-absolute prediction (of disease, earthquakes) and control will be possible.

Serious and objective historians, sociologists, and philosophers of science (Duane H. D. Roller, Ian Mitroff, and Thomas Kuhn, for example) sometimes have incisive or harsh things to say about what occurs in the entire scientific enterprise. Working scientists often react badly to these observations or criticisms. These are not the same unreasonable (irrational) postmodernist folks who denigrate science and foment science wars (consider Sandra Harding and her comment that Newton's *Principia Mathematica* is a "rape manual"; see Chapter 7 for further discussion). Far removed from the madness of postmodernist criticism is a softer form found in Sue Rosser's female friendly science. Here, the differences are primarily to be found in how human activities are managed rather than in procedure, which should be consistent, although the Nobelist Barbara McClintock used an intuitive approach and spoke of "a feeling for the organism" in her genetic botanical work.

It took scientists in conjunction with the federal government many years to come up with an acceptable definition of scientific misconduct. These folks were probably afraid of stepping on too many corrupt toes and so things such as cooking or trimming data, ignoring laboratory protocols, conflicts of interest, uninformed consent, or harassment are ignored. The big transgressions are falsification (distorting real data), fabrication (creating entirely imaginary data), and plagiarism (theft by failing to credit other's work).

For decades, as matters worsened especially in biomedicine, but in other hard sciences as well, physics, for example, scientists continued to deny that there was a problem. They reasoned that since there are tens of thousands of scientists producing millions of published results, a few abusers really do not have a meaningful effect. But these naive and overly loyal self-defenders and their professional organizations were wrong on both counts: Far more scientists commit misconduct than the profession is willing to admit even today and the results may lead to harm, illness, and death as the Wakefield/autism and Breuning/Sprague controversies attest. (See below and Chapter 6.)

The literature is replete with similar extravagances but these are merely the tip of the iceberg, the sensational instances that get media attention. Even monographic treatments of a series of historical cases such as *Betrayers of the Truth* (Broad) (and there are now many such overviews) or of just a single instance, *Plastic Fantastic* (Reich), fail to give a full measure of the scientists and medical practitioners who are guilty of misconduct. The sad truth probably is that most of these people remain hidden and continue to dissemble.

The Scope of Information Ethics

Twenty-two years ago, Alan Price published a revelatory article in the *Journal of Information Ethics* in which he outlines countless cases adjudicated by the Office of Research Integrity. Physicians, often with additional doctorates, purposely plagiarized, were found guilty, and were disciplined. The problem is that their punishments are laughable. For example, they were banned from applying for grants or acting as referees for three years. What is strikingly compelling is someone's observation that those who cheat are likely to repeat their crimes. They had proven untrustworthy, so they should be debarred for life from meaningful research through loss of license to practice medicine as well as a large fine and/or imprisonment. Marcel LaFollette, in *Stealing Into Print*, offers a litany of scientific plagiaries.

Perhaps the most infamous instance of misconduct in biomedicine (among many others including Robert Gallo, Eric Poehlman, Jon Sudbø, and Woo Suk Wang) is the *Cell*/Baltimore case. Here Margo O'Toole accused Thereza Imanishi-Kari and the Nobelist David Baltimore, as a coauthor, of malfeasance. The case dragged on and many people wrote accounts, critiques, and defenses, but ultimately it came down to failure to record scrupulously. Naturally, O'Toole came off badly. Very few malefactors admit their crimes. This, like most other such instances of scientific misconduct, was inherently harmful but did not have dire consequences for others or for society in general. But the very worst instance did and continues to do so: This concerns Andrew Wakefield, a medical doctor who is widely considered to have caused misery and death. He performed a trial and published the results in *The Lancet*, one of the most influential medical journals. They seemed to imply that the measles (MMR) vaccine was a *direct* cause of autism. But what *The Lancet* editors seemed to miss or ignore was that his sample consisted of just 12 children, which is essentially meaningless for inductive, statistical, generalizable conclusions. But even worse is that there was alleged fraud involved. People stopped vaccinating their children and the resurgence of measles resulted in illness and fatalities.

Very infrequently, the malefactor does get what he fully deserves and then ironically, we may end up feeling sorry for him. This was the case with Jan Hendrick Schön. Eugenie Samuel Reich details this serial falsifier's story in an overly detailed account. Schön published countless fraudulent papers in the very best journals, but it took a long time for his crimes to come to light. He did pay a price; he lost his wonderful job at Bell Labs and his university revoked his doctorate.

Scientific fraud is rampant because ethical training and commitment is lacking. Normative values inherent in a given discipline are inculcated as a student progresses through high school, college, doctoral, and post-doctoral work. Different laboratories may stress different necessities, but there is a core set of values that inhere in astronomical work (don't crack the mirror), chemistry (don't confuse H2O with H2SO4), and so on. Keep accurate records, data, and lab logs, do not cheat, steal, hack, or malign, harass, or abuse fellow researchers are probably preached at every level and in every discipline. But apparently all of this is inadequate. The most egregious ethical and legal lapses occur in computer science, where hacking and cracking may have led students to the field in the first place. Indeed, sophisticated knowledge here allows one to get an excellent job with surveillance agencies or to earn a living lifting funds from banking systems. If Americans are guilty, other nationals are more so, and the experts from some countries (Pakistan, Israel, Russia) are notorious for their cracking skills. And programmers and coders are especially at risk here and they have certainly succumbed at times either unknowingly or purposely. The results have been extremely harmful as the Volkswagen debacle shows. But, of course, there exist people with integrity who refuse to act unethically even when offered a remunerative opportunity. Bizarre as it may appear, some scientists seem unsure of what is acceptable. Researchers interviewed 48 physicists and discovered that ethical ambiguity confuses them. "[A]ltruism, inconsequential outcomes, and preserving the status quo" may result in unethical activity (Johnson, D. R.). The solution to all problems, as usual, is two-fold: more extensive ethical education* and a more draconian legal force to deal with those who

---

*Many years ago, when the present author had not yet retired from his academic position, he suggested to the dean of the graduate school (at a university that had 16,000 students) that the graduate school should sponsor a required university-wide course in ethical sensitization. Ethical malfeasance is not limited to the five hard sciences and their progeny including engineering, computer science, and agriculture. Perhaps if those who had seriously studied applied plant biology had considered ethical implications more carefully, we would not be inundated with genetically modified seeds and foods and pesticide applications; meat production would be reduced, and organic farming would be increased, not because of consumer demand but rather because it is an ethical agricultural alternative.

choose to cause harm to their disciplines, fellow human beings, and themselves.

See the Office of Research Integrity site http://ori.hhs.gov/ori-intro for elucidating materials including summaries of adjudicated misconduct cases and http://ori.hhs.gov/sites/default/files/rcrintro.pdf for Nicholas H. Steneck's ORI *Introduction to the Responsible Conduct of Research,* a comprehensive and useful guide to correct procedure. The spring 1996 number of the *Journal of Information Ethics* is devoted to "Research Misconduct" (primarily in science).

6   Social Science

"I was a magician. I created my own reality, and everyone thought it was real."—Diederik Stapel

The hard sciences do not have a monopoly on misconduct; the social sciences also perpetrate unethical activity. The most egregious general transgression is the claim on the part of many scholars in these fields (and shared even by some deranged humanists) that economics or anthropology is a science. Most notable here is psychology, where scientific recognition appears to be more important than judicious practice. These theorists and practitioners think that by appropriating the methodological trappings of astronomy, they turn their sometimes pseudoscientific beliefs into a rigorous controlled enterprise they pretentiously call science. The highly respected physicist Richard Feynman compared this to a cargo cult (Witkowski 93).

The psychological and economics disciplines are riddled not only with inherent problems that derive from dealing with unpredictable humans and animals, but their practitioners, especially in the therapeutic professions, promulgate harmful nonsense. The five hard sciences are more or less successful at deriving data from precisely regulated experiments and ultimately in predicting and controlling. The social sciences do a very bad job here, unable to replicate survey results because different people react differently. They also lie, whereas particles, elements, astronomical bodies, bacteria, and lava do not. An attempt to replicate 100 earlier psychological experiments failed in fewer than 50 percent of the cases. And Tom Bartlett offers an overly-lengthy account of Amy Cuddy's claim that power-posing (standing strong like Wonder Woman) alters one's self-confidence. Replication failed. Even her coauthor eventually balked despite the real fame and fortune that followed in the wake of this foolish and simplistic idea. It is a superb example of "psychological (pseudo)science."

Anthropologists subsidized military operations (lawyers defended exploiting prisoners), and, as M. Gregg Bloche points out, psychologists and even doctors accommodated and furthered torture, a reprehensible thing for a physician to do. Derek Freeman unfairly and falsely castigated Margaret Mead's Samoan research. Psychologists are notorious for their foibles, and Tomasz Witkowski and Maciej Zatonski, in *Psychology Gone Wrong*, provide readers with innumerable cases. They insist that the early proponents of IQ testing, as well as some later scholars who should have known better, were responsible for horrible things including the Holocaust and mass sterilizations that flowed out of the eugenics movement. Their data were incorrect and the prejudices of these men led them astray. The information failed them and people died, were pronounced feeble-minded, lost their rights, and were surgically decimated (22–24).

Cyril Burt, one of the twentieth century's most important and influential psychologists, was guilty of fabricating data (and imaginary assistants) in order to continually confirm his contention that intelligence is heritable. There can be little doubt that we come equipped with an inherited intelligence, but Burt carried this to an unacceptable and unproven extreme. Robert Sprague, a good and caring man, blew the whistle on Stephen Breuning and paid a price for his honesty and dedication (he lost his federal grant for the first time in 20 years; whistleblowers generally fare badly). Breuning claimed that treating hyperactive, mentally challenged children with specific medications had positive effects. His research was fraudulent and vulnerable children may have been hurt. Witkowski notes that he was sentenced to 60 days, probation, a small fine. and a few other things. For a time he sold electronic equipment (38–39).

Diederik Stapel, a Dutch social psychologist, published more than 50 impressive and influential papers, many of which caught the attention of the media because of the astounding discoveries that he made (people who eat meat are selfish and less social) but much of his work was completely fabricated including the surveys* that he ostensibly administered.

*Survey research is not scientific in the way that a chemistry experiment is. As noted, this is the problem with the social sciences generally, where psychology is the most pretentious and culpable.

He lost his doctorate, job, honor, dignity, and self-esteem. He wanted to be a super-star and ended up disdained and depressed. Stapel, though guilty of producing falsified or fabricated papers published in the most prestigious journals (Stapel) (which shows how ineffective peer review can be), probably caused less real harm than Breuning, whose fabricated work was detrimental.*

The torture mentioned above is an extremely controversial issue: After the World Trade Center bombing, some psychologists advocated and defended torture practically and on ethical grounds. William O'Donohue and his coauthors present a detailed argument concerning "psychologists' putative involvement with enhanced interrogations and torture [EIT]." First, their role here is not merely putative but acknowledged. Second, the authors' conclusion that "contra the American Psychological Association ... reasonable arguments can be made that in certain cases the use of EITs is ethical and even, in certain circumstances, morally obligatory..." is an abrogation of all that Americans hold dear: respect, dignity, and integrity. And third, the authors insist that there is "an ethical duty" to protect the psychologists alleged to be involved..." (abstract). They were not merely alleged. And they acted injudiciously. The O'Donohue paper is a disconcerting attempt to renounce ethical commitment.

Case after case unfolds and there is no need to multiply examples. It is, however, necessary to indicate the harm that therapists do. There are so many competing therapies (almost 500: Witkowski 159) that it is surprising that any of them are effective, especially since according to Witkowski, they are often founded in sand (109) and practitioners are problematic: "...charlatans, megalomaniacs and even sadists lurk among therapists in great numbers" (107). (This harsh judgment may be hyperbolic.)

Freud created his theories from personal experience and falsified or fabricated his data and so the entire psychoanalytic enterprise is questionable. Freud had some incisive ideas and they help to explain social, cultural, and individual motivations, but he also went badly astray.

---

*Yet worse, of course, was Wakefield's faulty medical research that resulted in severe harm and death. See Chapter 4 for more details.

Feminists are particularly dissatisfied with many of his insights. The Oedipus complex and penis envy are highly improbable etiological bases for the misery that follows for far too many people. Jung too managed to extrapolate too broadly from his mythic and archetypal conjectures. The therapies that derive from all of the early theoretical nonsense are highly questionable except as a catharsis for the person who enjoys and profits from pure articulation. In addition, Witkowski and Zatonski discuss negative aspects of childhood trauma, recovered memories, fabricated diseases, and unregulated therapists, a real therapeutic mess.

7 Humanities

Ron Robin, in his wonderful *Scandals and Scoundrels*, observes that there exists a general decline in the liberal arts, where "hoax, plagiarism, and misrepresentation" especially in history and anthropology can be found (4).

Naturally, scholars who work in the liberal arts, humanistic disciplines such as art history, philosophy, and musicology, are prone to cut corners, infuse their work with misleading, superfluous, or false ideological nonsense, or plagiarize (see this writer's *Authorial Ethics*, where various disciplines are covered in great detail), and no area is as guilty of creating untenable theories that then go on to wreak havoc generally, as theoretical literary criticism, whose heyday during the latter part of the twentieth century is now thankfully past.

A scholar who devotes his or her life to Rembrandt or Bach or the rococo is bound to come up with specific ideas or theories concerning work habits or methodologies, influences or patrons, decoration or style. Extrapolations based on historical evidence may be tenable but sometimes a person gets carried away. Some of these crackpot ideas are so outlandish that they are little known: Poe was murdered; Lewis Carroll was Jack the Ripper. But others take hold and many otherwise sane people come to believe, for example, that the Stratfordian Shakespeare did not write "Shakespeare's" plays (for additional examples, see Moore) or, in another context, that HIV does not cause AIDS, a notion debunked and rejected by the medical community.

Deconstruction, a subset of the postmodernist attitude (which might retrospectively come to include abstract expressionism), is the most egregious manifestation of the literary critic's compulsion to create bizarrely indefensible nonsense couched in inscrutable jargon. It is astonishing that scrupulous scholars at institutions around the world have been taken in by the resulting hokum (perhaps because they were afraid to be left behind or because the most prestigious journals would reject their work if they did not kowtow to the Yale Mafia's jabberings). Depending on the particular practitioner, the conjecturings, couched in absolutes, were foolish, ideologically stilted, incomprehensible, or false.

Postmodernist ideological criticism of science reached such a pitch that a dissenter decided to do something about it. Alan Sokal, a New York University physicist, wrote "Transgressing the Boundaries," an article defending some of the most bizarre claims of postmodernist thought, including a questioning of gravity. The editors of *Social Text*, a mouthpiece for the movement, were so elated to have a contribution from a legitimate scientist who apparently sympathized with its preachings, that it did not bother to vet the paper. What many people do not realize is that Sokal did not merely write the piece; instead, he lifted actual statements from the work of many of the movement's famous stars.

Approximately simultaneously with the paper's publication, a second piece appeared in *Lingua Franca*. Here Sokal explained that the *Social Text* paper was a hoax, a satire (of gibberish) created in order to expose and debunk the foolishness that postmodernism exports. Subsequently, a large body of literature on the Sokal hoax emerged, much of it written by Sokal himself. What are often ignored here are the ethical aspects of what he did: He created a paper that by its very existence gives a false impression despite the fact that all of its utterances can be found in the works of its cited authors including Donna Haraway, Jacques Lacan, Bruno Latour, Jean-François Lyotard, and others. Additionally, he tricked, fooled, and embarrassed the *Social Text* editors who, though guilty of scholarly distortion, probably did not deserve this harsh (and unethical) lesson.

Twenty years have passed but the hoax still inspires and irritates. In early 2017, *The Chronicle of Higher Education* published a group interview with positive and negative comments from many of the (peripherally) involved people. (Serious scientists, whose life work is generally denigrated by cultural critics, relish Sokal's work but others are defensive.) Alex Star, the editor of *Lingua Franca,* was unsure that publication had been ethically warranted (Ruark B8). Editors of *Social Text* are naturally incensed at the

---

deceptive "breach of ethics" (B8). But most culpable here are those critics who continue to come up with excuses for the foolishness of their anti-scientific nonsense: Science is just a cultural construct, and but one way of comprehending the world (DNA analysis and forensic anthropology, one might imagine—as opposed to astrology and shamanism?).

Stephen Hilgartner offers a weak defense by complaining that Sokal lumps diverse thinkers together and this is not "intellectually or ethically justifiable" and then deflects matters by calling up Rush Limbaugh and George Will as welcome recipients of Sokal's parody (B9). Worse is Stanley Fish's remark: The Sokal hoax provides fodder for those whose ignorance of postmodernism allows them to merely cite Sokal in order to dismiss its project (B9). One would have thought that Fish could do better than that. The upshot is that Sokal succeeded in debunking; the postmodernists were exposed; and the *Social Text* editors were embarrassed.

Historians may falsify or fabricate, sometimes only for the pleasure of perpetrating a prank and fooling readers by creating counterknowledge. But Michael Bellesiles seriously fabricated data in his acclaimed study *Arming America;* the Bancroft Prize which he garnered was retracted and he lost his job (Hauptman, *Authorial* 46–47). More ubiquitous is plagiarism, which in the history discipline is easy to accomplish. There exists an enormous body of work on the topic and the spring and fall 1994 issues of the *Journal of Information Ethics* are devoted to plagiary generally and the Stephen Oates case in particular. Oates was accused of failing to fully indicate his sources in *With Malice Toward None,* his well-received Lincoln biography. This created a major controversy and harmed Oates and probably some of his accusers as well ("Plagiarism").

Excluding the purposeful, sometimes propagandistic deceptions that riddle the Internet, the most blatantly fabricated work occurs in art and, to a lesser extent, literature. In the former area, technically skilled artists create paintings (and prints), pass them off as original Vermeers or Matisses and sell them for enormous sums of money. Han van Meegeren and Elmyr de Hory come immediately to mind. That this can occur is due exclusively to the authentication process. No one lays out $50 million for an artwork until a group of physical and technological experts indicate that this really is an undiscovered, provenance-free Dürer. One might wonder where it has been for the past 500 years.

Physical authentication allows an expert in the artist's style to compare and contrast and this includes not just style and brushstroke, but also canvas and stretchers, framing and materials, labels and markings. Then the technologically adept analyze the paints' chemical constituents, the hair left from a brush, and so on, using various techniques including imaging systems. In this way, the work can be dated if, for example, no chromium pigment was available before 1800 and it turns up in abundance in a work purported to be from 1500. These experts make many mistakes!

In late 2016, Sotheby's rescinded a sale of Frans Hals's "Portrait of a Man," which turned out be a modern forgery. The many authenticators were wrong, although some experts continue to fight for its authenticity (Siegal C1). These experts earn their living by authenticating works. They are human and can be swayed by carelessness, desire, fame, and money. Here, information is misapplied because of unethical or illegal ineptitude or dishonesty. The end result is that purchasers suffer emotional and monetary harm, forgeries contaminate the historical record, and a single person earns a lot of undeserved money. (Perhaps among the more astonishing cases is that of an elderly, twentieth century, Dutch painter, who, many years before, had painted a series of works. A forged painting purported to be from that series was brought to him and he authenticated it, regaling the messenger with a prurient story concerning his model.)

Provenances are also affirmed by creating documents for the fake paintings; sometimes an expert mistakenly confirms but often a document is merely forged. In late 2016, a well-known dealer in antiquities was arrested. She dealt with authentic objects "plundered" from Indian and Cambodian holy sites; they were stolen and then sold illegally. Nancy Wiener managed this "by creating fraudulent documents" which deceived buyers, who thought that what they purchased had a very different provenance. Works that she sold are in major museums around the world, although some may have been legitimately acquired (Mashberg). It seems reasonable that many of the purchasers would not have spent millions of dollars had they known that these artifacts were stolen and smuggled into the United States.

In literature, forgeries occur—including James Macpherson's Ossian poems and Konrad Kujau's Hitler diaries—but here things can be more complex than mere forgery. For example, Lee Israel did indeed forge letters that she attributed to famous authors and sold them to credulous dealers, but hers was an extremely convoluted plot that included purchasing many typewriters with different fonts and actually stealing correspondence from the New York Public Library's extraordinary collection, copying it, and then returning the copy to the library so that she was able to sell the original. Very different from forgery, Laura Albert not only conceived the fabricated character JT LeRoy, who authored powerful and highly praised works such as *Sarah*, she actually had someone impersonate Leroy at gatherings. This monumental hoax eventually disintegrated. A well-received cinematic version, *Author: The JT LeRoy Story*, was released in 2016. A poverty-stricken woman shoplifts in order to feed her children and may be severely embarrassed and punished; depending on matters, she might even lose her children. But these intellectual thieves cause a great deal of physical, financial, and emotional harm, by spreading misinformation through space and time (Corot painted 3,000 works and 5,000 of them are in the United States!) but are not adequately punished. Thomas Mallon, in *Stolen Words*, offers a general overview of literary plagiarism.

Finally, composers are notorious for quoting the works of their peers. A piece of popular Korean music, Topp Dogg's "Top Dog" begins with a long excerpt from Mozart's 25th symphony (K. 183); it is a peculiar listening experience. Shostakovich quotes Beethoven's *Wellington's Victory* in his *Battle Symphony*. Since these composers are not around to make a fuss, it is apparently okay. This is not the case with popular songs, a category that includes music played on the radio, alternative rock, and esoteric, often vulgar material only offered via the Internet. Here quotation is subtle, and sometimes inadvertent; that is, a song composer heard something in the distant past and it remained in his subconscious. It sneaked into his new hit, even though he did not realize it. But the original composer did. And so he or she sometimes hires a forensic musicologist to ferret out the truth. "Blurred Lines" cost Robin Thicke and his co-writer 7.4 million dollars, which Marvin Gaye's estate gladly accepted. An earlier famous case had George Harrison's "My Sweet Lord" indebted to the Chiffons' wonderful "He's So Fine." (See Lynch for additional examples.) Not all musical quotation derives from innocent error. Plagiary is profitable. It is also unethical and in some cases illegal.

8   Peer Review, Publication, Retraction

Peer Review

Peer review is a process that has long outlived its usefulness. Although this author disagrees that it is a form of censorship, it is certainly guilty of many other informational harms, while often failing in its appointed tasks, which are to cull out the best work for editors of both journals and scholarly monographs (as well as for grant proposals) and simultaneously, when working well, to offer suggestions to anxiously awaiting authors, whose academic or laboratory careers may depend on the reviewers' decisions. Peer review is an excessively cumbersome, inefficient, and time consuming process that requires editors to send out multiple copies of a paper in hard copy or now more frequently in digital format to specific scholars whose expertise equips them for the job of scrupulously evaluating the appropriateness and quality of the paper for the particular journal or the publisher's monographic line.

A superb paper on kinesthetic responses to various nutritional stimuli would be rejected out of hand by *New Literary History* and, concomitantly, "John Donne's Influence on Dylan Thomas" would not go over well at *Cell*. But what occurs when an iconoclastic scholar tries to show that Emily Brontë's fiction is overwrought, stilted, and tedious is that few competent reviewers would allow this to pass. Even if the paper were superb and fully documented (that is, the author proves the case), most academics would fear for their reputations and the editor of *Victorian Studies* or *PMLA* would have to be a senior scholar to risk the wrath of his or her colleagues. Peer review stifles creativity.

8. Peer Review, Publication, Retraction

Because the entire process presents so many problems for editors, software has been designed to allow contributors to submit their papers electronically and to track the paper through its peregrinations. This benefits editors but makes life difficult for the contributor who must spend 30 minutes registering and then more time trying (unsuccessfully) to upload the work. The rest of the traditional process remains intact: Editors must locate reviewers, send them the work, and then wait for their responses; sometimes they wait an eternity.

Next comes the need to communicate the results to the author, require a revised version, and possibly have the piece reevaluated by a new set of peer reviewers. Months, years, decades pass. It is no exaggeration to say that at times, the finally accepted paper is dated, and there still remain months until it actually appears. With online (open access) publication, things may have speeded up a bit. At the *Journal of Information Ethics* (which this author edits), it takes between one and two years from acceptance to publication, and peer review does not play a role here.

The measure of how all of this works can be seen in two personal experiences. A colleague and I submitted a complex paper to a prestigious journal. The wait was interminable; after about six months, we inquired and discovered that the editor could not think of a competent reviewer, so he let the paper sit on top of a filing cabinet. A day after our initial contact, he called back and accepted the piece, so it appeared in a refereed publication without being reviewed. Worse, I once observed a stressed reviewer open a paper, glance at it, and reject it immediately without turning a page; this was very unfair to the author(s).

Reviewers expend (waste) an astonishing amount of time evaluating material. "The mean hours per manuscript" spent by thousands of reviewers varies from little more than one hour to as many as six. Some do as many as 22 manuscripts per year. The value of the findings, however, in many thousands of reviews (one radiology journal produced almost 18,000 peer reviews) was by and large positive. In blinded cases, in 2,000 reviews, authors were identifiable some 33 percent of the time and in one journal's 312 reviews, this reached 83 percent (Weller 156, 168, 216). Ann C. Weller concludes her survey by insisting that peer review "is essential to the integrity of scientific and scholarly communication" (322). This author is skeptical.

Reviewers are human so they too often act in a typically human way; here follows a limited list: They subvert the review process; restrict the flow of information, as David Shatz points out (30); may be biased; fail to do their job in a timely manner; offer unhelpful, unreasonable, mistaken, crotchety, nasty, or abusive advice; stifle creativity; negate work so that their own can take precedence; steal ideas; fail to make judicious evaluations; and almost never root out fabrication, falsification, plagiary, cooking and trimming of data, conflicts of interest, and other sordid, unethical actions. Richard Smith, former editor of *BMJ* (*British Medical Journal*), "inserted major errors" into papers and quite a few reviewers never caught all of them and some found none (89); he also insists that the consensus among reviewers on a specific paper is barely better than one would expect to occur by chance (84).

This is a system most appropriate in the hard sciences; it slipped into gear in psychology, anthropology and their kin because these disciplines like to emulate chemistry and geology, and not to be outdone, literary and philosophical editors decided to follow suit. As I have long insisted, a competent editor in almost any field and certainly those in pointed sub-disciplines (perhaps excluding the five hard sciences and mathematics) will be able to make an evaluative decision on his or her own. If not, he or she should probably find another career.

It may be unfair to criticize peer review for something it is not meant to accomplish, but one really has little choice: Weeding out fraudulent work would seem to be far more important than judging a paper to be marginally acceptable for a prestigious publication. If *Nature* accepts a shoddy piece of scholarship, whose statistical conclusions are flawed because the author cannot differentiate a chi-square result from a square root, it is lamentable, but forgivable. But if the editors of the very best social psychology journals publish some 50 fraudulent papers that Stapel authored over an extended period, this is a debacle of extraordinary magnitude. All of those peer reviewers failed and failed again to root out wholesale falsification and fabrication. Indeed, and even more horrifying, his many collaborators, both colleagues and graduate students, also failed to note that things were amiss. Now their reputations are sullied by association. This is not helpful in a tight academic market.

Critics have submitted purposely fabricated or distorted papers or manuscripts to journals or publishers in order to test peer review and editorial acumen. Both failed. In 1979, an experimenter resubmitted Jerzy Kosinsky's National Book Award winning novel *Steps* to 14 prestigious publishers including the company that had brought it out. All 14 rejected the manuscript! In 1982, Douglas Peters and Stephen Ceci presented the results of an experiment in which they chose 12 published articles, made slight alterations, and resubmitted them to the original, prestigious psychology journals. "Of the sample of 38 editors and reviewers, only three (8 percent) detected the resubmissions." Of the remaining nine articles, eight were rejected. This appears to be impossible, since the refereed papers had been accepted less than three years earlier. The editors did not recognize the articles and the new set of referees drew very different conclusions concerning their quality. Somehow, "serious methodological flaws" had infected the papers.

In 2013, John Bohannon offered a gravely error-riddled piece to some 300 open access publications. More than half accepted it. In a paper sponsored by and published in *Science,* which, along with *Nature,* is the most prestigious general scientific periodical, Bohannon explained in great detail what he had done; he indicates problems with peer review not only at predatory but also at legitimate open access publications: "The paper was accepted by journals hosted by industry titans Sage and Elsevier. The paper was accepted by journals published by prestigious academic institutions such as Kobe University in Japan. It was accepted by scholarly society journals. It was even accepted by journals for which the paper's topic was utterly inappropriate, such as *the Journal of Experimental & Clinical Assisted Reproduction.*" The editors also assessed payments, minimal amounts such as $90 and exorbitant bribes such as $3,100, typical even of highly respected publications; but they often do not indicate this necessity until much later: these are "deceptive open-access journals 'parasitizing the scientific research community.'" This process for confirming the worth and value of publishable papers is horribly flawed, since "The most basic obligation of a scientific journal is to perform peer review," which often fails dismally or does not occur at all.

These kinds of fraudulent inquiries are useful because they provide evidence of a problematic and defective system, but they also are unethical because they are deceptive, trick people, and waste the time of bogus but also legitimate, hard working editors and reviewers. At least since 1982, David Horrobin has been criticizing peer review, which "...is a **non-validated charade** [bold in original] whose processes generate results little better than does chance" (2). Despite all of this, peer review continues to roll along on its appointed though flawed and misleading path, and despite the fact that some commentators call for its termination.

The crisis in peer review is so pressing that the *Journal of the American Medical Association (JAMA)* sponsors a quadrennial conference, which in its earliest manifestations, reasonably enough, emphasized biomedical matters but now has broadened its scope to include other disciplines. Many hundreds of papers on peer review have been presented by medical personnel who would, under normal circumstances, be better off serving their constituency by discussing hematology or neurology, schistosomiasis or how to reduce the number of hours a resident must work in the emergency room. (See the fall 1998 issue of the *Journal of Information Ethics*, which is devoted to the subject ["Peer Review"]).

Publication

The goal of virtually all writers is to get their research results, fiction, or poetry into print, whether in hard copy or online or both. Occasionally, an author writes for herself, and so it was with D. who composed novel after novel and stored them in a trunk. This was apparently creation as catharsis, but it is very rare indeed. This is not to be confused with those people who write, attempt to publish, fail, and give up. Even today, when vanity presses can bring out anyone's detritus or one can visit a bookstore that owns a printing device, and walk out an hour or two later with bound copies of his or her magnum opus, publication can be an onerous task: locating an agent; submitting material; receiving rejections; encountering unreasonable contractual demands and subsequent abrogations; waiting interminably for the work to appear; and sometimes being dissatisfied with the exorbitant payments one must make in some disciplines and open access, the version produced, the marketing, or the royalties doled out.

Ethical problems occur on both sides of the divide: Editors and publishers cause harm and writers take short cuts. This author presented a contracted manuscript to a publisher. The text was excellent, but the ca.

100 contracted images, which were an integral part of the book, were expunged by people whose graphic standards were unreasonably high. This ruined the book for the author who had spent two years composing it. His coauthor may not feel quite as strongly, but he too undoubtedly misses the illustrations. Editors fail to respond in a timely fashion; accept and then reject material; discourteously mistreat writers; require difficult to implement submission methods, revisions, and timelines; and mistakenly share ostensibly confidential data. They also act in an egregiously unethical way when they insist that authors cite the editor's journal or work in order to appear in his or her pages.

The present author has more than once considered (and threatened) a suit when purposely harmed by uncaring editors. One would have been pursued in Paris against the United Nations; it seemed like a foolish waste of time, energy, and money. Another threat managed to achieve its end, though the editor tortured him by questioning almost every articulation and demanding countless revisions in order to discourage him from continuing. He obliged and the piece ultimately appeared in a prestigious periodical.

Authors do many things that cause harm including lie, cheat, plagiarize, abuse colleagues and students (in an academic environment), fail to cite or cite correctly, manipulate images, propagandize for a corporation's products even though he or she receives payment from the company—and there is more, a painful litany of misdeeds. Traditional publication presents a specific set of problems, online another. In the former system one could present work in two basic ways, periodical or monographic dissemination.

Negative possibilities abound: In 2002, for example, many scientists indicated that an Elsevier journal, *Regulatory Toxicology and Pharmacology*, was not a refereed publication but rather an "industry mouthpiece." The writers work for the companies that then allude to the articles in order to change the minds of regulators (Guterman).

Online, one has many choices: personal or general websites or blogs; letters or comments appended to published material; magazines and journals; and a variety of social media. Some of the posted material is vetted, some not at all. One of the most popular sources is not especially reliable: Though it is not its purpose and it frowns upon it, *Wikipedia* does allow authors to dissemble, distort, and harm in many ways. The checks and balances help to dissuade the inclusion of misinformation, but one can be certain that there is considerably more detritus in *Wikipedia* than in a traditional reference tool that has been carefully vetted by editors who almost never have a stake in the entry, precisely the antithesis of the way authors function in this online encyclopedia. See the "Publishing Ethics" issue of the *Journal of Information Ethics* (Spring 1997).

Retraction

As noted, *The Times* publishes corrections; so too do journals, which may include errata slips in subsequent issues, as once did second printings of scholarly books. When the problems or errors are extreme, one or more of the authors can formally retract a paper, which, analogous to annulment, implies that it was never published, though there it still is! When there are multiple authors, sometimes, absurdly, as many as a thousand, they may not all agree, and this presents an insurmountable hurdle. When authors are loath to retract something that is truly egregious, the journal's editor can intervene and do so instead. This obviously creates an unpleasant situation, made especially horrendous if it eventually turns out that the paper is valid. And, finally, an editor can retract without notifying the author, which is both highly discourteous and unethical.

Retraction has become big business and papers that undergo this disastrous fate are now so marked in indices and across the paper. But searching modalities have changed and instead of indices such as the *Modern Language Association Bibliography* or *Medline,* researchers now can use Google or Google Scholar or they can search directly on the website of the periodical or in an aggregated collection such as JSTOR or use an agglomerated online index such as Elsevier's Scopus or even Academic Search Premier. Thus, in some cases, the retraction will not be visibly noted and some retracted papers continue to ripple through the scholarly literature. Some years ago, retractions became so meaningful that two medical editors started *Retraction Watch* (retractionwatch.com) which concentrates on the scientific literature, including psychology and especially biomedicine, because that is where the retractions take place. Very few critical analyses of Daniel Defoe's novels or Gerard Manley Hopkins' poetry are retracted.

8. Peer Review, Publication, Retraction

Papers are retracted because they have been found to be misleading, riddled with errors of various types, or the result of misconduct (falsification, fabrication, plagiarism). The Committee on Publication Ethics (COPE) calls for retraction only for error, misconduct, redundant publication, and research breaches (Wager 1). But since means do not justify ends, many other misdeeds could be grounds for retraction including (financial) conflicts of interest, failure to obtain IRB approval or informed consent, purposely harming animal and human subjects and so on. But it is improbable that these "minor" infractions lead to retraction with any frequency, since it constitutes waste, is embarrassing, and besmirches the reputation(s) of the author(s).

9 Storage, Access, Provision

Storage

What was once a very simple matter, the storage of data and information, became increasingly complex as the twentieth century unfolded and new media and additional storage possibilities developed. No one visited an enemy in 1850 wearing a wire in order to record his nasty asseverations; that is because there were no wires, no recorders, no batteries, no available electric current. For three quarters of a century, it has been unequivocally illegal to record a phone conversation without a warrant. The advent of mobile devices, for some inexplicably esoteric reason, falls outside of that ruling and so intelligence agencies record everything—and save it: Print, audio, film—all are archived in various ways and the hardware for its reproduction is constantly superseded or lost.

Stored data and information is sometimes no longer accessible: The medium degenerates (like wax cylinders and celluloid film), and things cannot be listened to or viewed without appropriate machinery. There are stacks, micro-formats, CDs, online storage, clouds—it never ends. The entire run of government documents from the beginning of the depository system until 1984, when this author was on the faculty at the University of Oklahoma, was stored under the eaves of Bizzell Memorial Library. It is hot in Norman and the sun beat down year after year, searing these acidic papers. Few patrons desired or needed agricultural data or a pamphlet on window cleaning from 1897. If they had, the paper probably would have disintegrated in their hands. Now we store everything regardless of its value including tweets and texts and nasty interchanges; articles, scientific papers, and books; websites and blogposts (both of which come and go); and everything else. No one ever considers that not everything requires or deserves preservation, least of all the millions of conversations archived by the NSA and its sister agencies.

Physical storage also entails some unusual technological gimmickry that seduced those collection administrators who had vast sums of money to expend on, for example, robotic book collectors, something akin to the equipment employed by Amazonian enterprises to collect the junk that people order online. Even as a substitute for the roller skating pages in the hundreds of miles of closed stacks at the New York Public Library's research division, this would be an enormous waste of resources. In normal diminutive collections of just two or three million volumes, it would be insanity.

Now we arrive at the ethics of storage, a concept that initially will appear to be almost laughable, but as it happens, with only four exceptions (misconduct, cracking, surveillance, warfare), it is the single most salient potentially unethical area discussed in the present work. Exclusively digital professional storage includes anything of importance to government, business, and legal and medical facilities. If this is crucial data or information (military plans, finances, trial results, insulin history) and personnel have failed to back it up in many ways and it is lost to cracking, kidnapping, or crashing then a major informational catastrophe may ensue. (A hospital paid a ransom to retrieve its kidnapped data!) Or consider the plight of the librarian who spends millions of dollars on bundled digital journal subscriptions from companies like Elsevier and Springer. No hard copy of these many hundreds of publications exist on site. The collection has physical issues for thousands of journals that it has collected for 150 years stored in the basement or in an offsite facility, but it is now entirely dependent on the company's servers for recent back issues. What happens when it is necessary to cancel some (usually contractually illegal) or all of the bundled publications, and the company refuses access to the archived issues already paid for? And what occurs if the company ceases to exist? Well, everything may be lost.

The same thing obtains for those individuals who choose to store their precious documents, papers, and images in a cloud and the (nebulous) cloud clears and the material is lost? In all of these instances, a human being has failed to act ethically; he or she has not fully and completely protected a professional or personal interest. This author, for example, backs up this developing manuscript's file (when working, at a minimum, daily) with a duplicate computer file, an email copy sent to a server 1500 miles away, and the original file on an external, disconnected device (a thumb drive), which is not left in the computer in order to avoid contamination. In the early days of personal computing and for many years, he printed everything he keyed in, over and over again. Losing material is not an option!

Access

First and foremost, access implies that data and information are actually available, but often they are not. No one or only a select few can locate and benefit from government, corporate, and private material that the owner or producer does not wish to share at all or only with a limited number of persons. It is understandable that those who own and profit from copyrighted, patented, and secretive material would want to protect it and that is why some more altruistic people have created free magazines and other reading material, pretty good encryption, computer programs, software, real open access (not the type for which authors must pay), and websites that do not engage in fund raising of any kind.

Most guilty here is the government, which limits the flow of data and information by unnecessarily declaring non-secret material "Sensitive but Unclassified," "Limited Official Use," and 50 other such designations (Sarokin 186). A change would have immense benefits: "We have been making the case ... that freeing up the flow of information in the economic sphere makes for more robust, responsive, and sustainable economic activity. Might the same be true in national and international policy? Can better access to information, more or less on its own, promote the objectives of global-scale peace and security?" (Sarokin 189).

Second is controlled access. The really important stuff, the online papers that a researcher might need may only be available through an expensive library subscription or if one is willing to pay $30 for a few pages. Here is where the thieves come into play. And the archival material in collections—millions of linear feet of papers and manuscripts on shelves, in filing cabinets, and scrolls and incunabula all of which are not posted on the Internet: these require visits to the Morgan in New York or the Huntington in California, Saint Catherine's Monastery in the Sinai or the Mogao Grottoes near Dunhuang in China.

Access also necessitates mentioning the digital divide, which is really a subset of the informational divide that includes not merely a lack of equipment and financial support but also literacy and the ability to use electronic devices. Given that one is capable, not having the resources to own and access a device or a nearby facility such as a library in urban or rural America or Africa or China, those who can and may locate online data and information and thus have an insurmountable advantage over those who cannot and do not. It is easy to repeat clichés, but "information is power" is an incisive apothegm: Both humans and even animals who know prosper; those who do not die.

Provision

Libraries

Just a few years ago, it was often difficult and sometimes impossible for even a sophisticated and knowledgeable person to locate necessary apposite data and information. Potential sources were manifold, even when held in a single location such as a public or academic library, special or private collection, museum, or local or federal government facility or depository. All of these locations also exist in countries around the world.

Discovering and accessing certain materials required knowing that NUCMC exists (see, you never heard of it) and knowing how to use it. Next came the need to write letters to California or Germany or Japan and ask questions and make requests. This sometimes raised a secondary problem for mono-lingual Americans who do not speak German or Japanese. Luckily for English speakers, many though not all foreign professionals do have at least a passing acquaintance with English. Finally, one had to pay a visit to the location and seek help.

Even much simpler requests in public, academic, and special collections

---

required a librarian knowledgeable in academic subjects, business, law, or medicine. High school and college students were especially at risk, if left to their own devices. A student studying business might spend hours searching for key business ratios and never find what the instructor expected without some guidance. Reference librarians spent hundreds of hours learning about specific tools, systems, and databases and how to access them. A search for a specific molecule in a specific compound or drug would entail knowledge of how to use the hard copy or online version of *Chemical Abstracts*, and that was no easy task.

Today, things are very different. Not everything is on the Internet but a great deal is. Sometimes it is free. Sometimes there is no charge if one is affiliated with an institution and knows how to access the material rather than settling for the first screen to come up on a search engine. (Google is not the only useful way to attack a problem.) And having excellent unbiased critical acumen (something inculcated in both high school and college) helps one to differentiate and cull the truthfully useful from the trash. Sometimes things can be vey expensive and most people, let alone impecunious students, will not be willing to pay $30 for a two page article. (This is why appropriating Sci-Hub is able to flourish.) It is still probable that a hard copy atlas will offer a much more useful map, depending on various factors, but most people will settle for a tiny Google version on a diminutive computer or smart phone screen because it is convenient. This merely mimics what occurred when road atlases replaced geographically diverse foldable maps, one, for example, that laid out all of New England rather than just Maine.

Archives

The commitment of librarians is to the free and unfettered provision of help and information. That is why this author's 1976 experiment was and is so powerful. That professionals in both public and academic collections were helpful in providing information on cordite to show how one might blow up a suburban home, something he made patently clear, was a misdirected gesture of a misguided professionalism (Hauptman "Professionalism"). Things have changed. This has always been the antithesis in archival work where the professional mandate is not broad and unthinking dissemination but rather protection of both the collected material and the legacy of those so chronicled.

Archivists offer many reasons to forestall access. They collect, arrange, catalogue, and create finding aids, and advertise their wares, but may refuse access to anyone deemed dangerous or unreliable or not acceptable to donors and for any other reason, especially if a valuable collection has been tendered with very precise and binding provisos. Here is where digitization may help, at least in some cases: Collections available on the Internet may be more accessible to those who might be denied at a physical location. In libraries, access is paramount; in special collections (of invaluable, unique, irreplaceable material) and in archives, protection is the highest priority. All of this does not mean that archivists consistently stifle research, but provision is certainly handled differently here.

For some reason archives (termed "the archive" in intellectual circles) have become a popular topic, perhaps because this is where the crucial data, information, and evidence lie (but they always have) for researchers attempting to discover the truth about, well, everything. For example, *Social Text*, the journal previously devoted to postmodernist nonsense and the butt of the Sokal hoax (see Chapter 7), offers an entire issue on "The Question of Recovery: Slavery, Freedom, and the Archive" ("The Question"). But this does not mean that archivists share willingly, although it is irresponsible and unethical to block researchers from discovering truths that may put people (and kings) in a bad light. Astonishingly, this is the reigning policy at the Royal Archives housed at Windsor Castle, where the material is exempt from freedom of information requests and those fortunate few who do enter are searched in a bathroom upon leaving. Requested files are refused and potential publications are vetted and censored. The truth is concealed and the public, not having the full story, becomes suspicious and believes foolishness (Baird).

And in rare instances, even libraries stifle access, but for good reason. Fifty years ago, a legitimate researcher could visit the British Library and request the Beowulf manuscript or the Lindisfarne Gospels and there they were! For a specialist or bibliophile, this was as close to heaven as they were likely to get. Today, the originals are not available. In order to protect these unique and priceless documents, they are no longer shared individually but rather displayed.* Instead, a true facsimile is presented. Here, the term is used precisely; what this means is that everything, including wormholes, in the original is reproduced with exactitude. Still, as on a palimpsest, something might not shine through in the copy that would be observable in the original. (Heather MacNeil's *Without Consent* offers an excellent overview of archival accessibility. See also the spring 2010 issue of *JIE*, which is devoted to "Archival Ethics: New Views"; the extraordinary papers in that issue cover repatriation of Indian artifacts, secret church material, and Heidegger's restricted papers, among many other topics.)

Government

In the United States, the federal government automatically provides information to its citizens (and anyone else, for that matter) through many programs and agencies. For example, NASA publishes an astonishing array of pamphlets, CDs, posters, and other items that are then given away to those who desire them. Much of what the government produces and publishes is shared with the public through depository collections often located within a university library (as is the separate NASA material). These facilities are staffed by a librarian who cares for the enormous physical and now online collection and guides people who wish to locate material.

Naturally some of the government's documents are controlled, hidden, or classified, and therefore not available, when they should be. It is for this reason that the Freedom of Information Act (FOIA) was passed into law. A desirous researcher files an FOIA request and an agency is supposed to honor it. And often it does. But sometimes it lags (especially when a president indicates that these requests should be handled in a

---

*Protection of unique artifacts is not merely warranted; it is the unequivocal responsibility and obligation of those who control them. Nevertheless, potential failures occur. Sometime in the early 1970s, this author accompanied the Museum of London's curator on a long automobile journey to Edinburgh, where they visited a collection in order to pick up a helm and psalter for a display at her museum. These items are so valuable that they were kept in a vault and were uninsurable. We placed them in the back of the station wagon and paid little attention to them as we meandered back to London. I spent the time worrying; the others were indifferent to their charges. Never leave anything in a car that you cannot afford to lose!

tardy manner). The agency may never reply and another request must be filed. The worst case scenario occurs when documents are shared, but parts or even all of the information has been blacked out because some functionary thought that no one should be privy to whatever it is that the document contains.

Information provision here is stifled and for no reason, since a very high percentage of "secret" data and information should never have been classified in the first place or the message, say, from the Civil War is no longer of any protective value. Now it could help historians understand something that has been sequestered for 150 years. There is such a hard copy backlog of materials that government document librarians will always be necessary to provide help; even online material including current law and legislative history may be impenetrable for many people.

10   Intellectual Freedom and Censorship

"...American democracy absolutely cannot survive a citizenry that can't tell the difference between what's true and what's false, that can't be bothered to find out, and that doesn't even think it matters."—Nancy Stark

When discussing rights, life and liberty are stressed and correctly so. The First Amendment to the Constitution protects against the abridgment of speech. But these things are nevertheless curtailed even in the United States, and naturally in many other locations and throughout history. The one thing that cannot be abrogated, even through a barrage of life-long propaganda, is *personal* intellectual freedom. It may be considered a right but it is more than that. It is similar to physiological functioning but on a mental level. Even the brainwashed may consider matters in a different light, though they never articulate them.

The normal human being in any society has the ability to process data and information, to think against the grain. It would be beneficial and laudable if this were truly carried over into social settings, but often this is impossible. In a closed religious community inhabited, for example, by the Amish or Hasidim, articulated free thought may result in expulsion. In a broader setting, such as the southern United States, speaking out against racial injustice, long ago or even today, could be painful. And in a constricted society such as Stalin's Soviet Union or North Korea, dissension can be life-threatening.

Americans, including those with factually contrary beliefs (Biblical literalism, anti-evolution), favor intellectual freedom. We do not like to be told what to do or what to believe. So we are free to think as we wish, read and view, and at least theoretically to articulate these thoughts, unless we are in Thailand or Saudi Arabia or unless someone attempts to censor us. The American Library Association's *Intellectual Freedom Manual* is an invaluable resource for "guiding principles and policies," on access, copyright, privacy, confidentiality, and so on, and not just for librarians and information professionals who are acculturated to protect intellectual freedom and rail against censorship. Anyone who respects the life of the mind would profit from its diverse content.

True democracy guarantees the freedom to think and promulgate, which in turn affirms and extends democratic ideals, and the Internet ostensibly enhances democracy; it probably does in some cases, such as the Arab spring especially in Tunisia, though not in Syria, most people would admit.

But the Internet is also a conduit for everything inimical to democracy: demagoguery, hate, libel, defamation, terror, evil. Evgeny Morozov claims that we are confused by cyber-utopianism and Internet-centrism; this "net delusion" not only does not promote democracy, it subverts it (xvii). And in a broader context and even more devastating, Susan Maret observes that "The tampering with communications through secrecy, propaganda, censorship, surveillance, or all techniques working as a complex of information control, influences historical understanding, social memory, and the fulfillment of human rights that support intellectual freedom" (266).

Living in a democracy has many advantages but also requires certain obligations such as the need to vote, which a high percentage (ca. 30–50 percent) of people abjure. Inhabiting the Internet is now a normal part of our lives but it does not demand anything. No one is obliged to act democratically because, as usual, ethical commitment is inadequate and the laws that do obtain in certain national venues have little enforcement power, especially in other lands. Despite protections, governmental, organizational, individual, and self-censorship continue to harass, control, and damage even its fiercest proponents.

Intellectual freedom implies free speech, and the freedom to speak exempt from governmental, political, or religious control is the hallmark of a democratic society, which the United States represents in its most potent form. Timothy Garton Ash indicates that speech should be free for self-realization, to locate the truth, for good government, and to help "live with diversity" (73–78). He goes on to discuss ten principles of free speech including expression, avoidance of violence, respect for religion, privacy, and an unencroached Internet (see http://freespeechdebate.com/en/).

Censorship is the denial of free speech and is anathema to anyone who cares about the life of the mind, the judicious dissemination and application of data, information, and knowledge, and ethical interaction with what we take to be the truth. There is no doubt that it is possible to call to mind historical necessities or imagined scenarios in which some form of censorship might be defensible. And indeed the Supreme Court has managed to come up with too many that at least superficially demand control. A famous if misleading example is shouting "Fire" in a crowded theater, when there is none and thereby causing a panicked attempt at escape, one that results in trampling, harm, and death. So, this is a case in which the government censors by making certain types of speech illegal, despite the Constitution's First Amendment. But applying this as a precedent, censors can come up with countless examples of similar necessities: private information (if any still exists), hate speech, secret government documents, libel, slander, and so on. And it is difficult to fault government for trying to protect citizens and its own secrets.

Nevertheless, one must be scrupulously careful or every individual, organization, religious group, and government bureaucrat will return to the past when the Bible, Dante, geocentric theories, Henry Miller, James Joyce, and pornography were ripe for censoring. The *Index Librorum Prohibitorum*, which obtained from the mid–16th century until 1966, allowed the Catholic church to ban books it did not like, and there were many it did not like. Banning continues to such an extent that every year Americans celebrate Banned Books Week. Consider that the following are typical fodder for censors: *Alice's Adventures in Wonderland, Candide, The Canterbury Tales, The First Circle, Fanny Hill, The Jungle, Rights of Man, Uncle Tom's Cabin,* and so on. Books are banned or censored because they offend, denigrate, are politically incorrect, offer positive perspectives on iconoclastic matters (such as homosexuality or drug use), affirm irreligious theories (such as evolution) or unscientific ones (such as intelligent design), feature obscenity or sexuality, articulate unpalatable political truths, and reveal evils. Recall the bizarre controversies concerning *Heather Has Two Mommies* (lesbianism) or *The Higher Power of Lucky* (because the word scrotum appears in a children's book).

Naturally, what is praiseworthy in the United States may be censored in China or Iran and the reverse obtains as well. The casual reader will expect that the overly religious or corrupt butchers* will be in the forefront of controlling thought, but Immanuel Velikovsky's *Worlds in Collision* brought the wrath of scientists down upon Macmillan, its publisher, which was threatened and probably lost business because of a boycott. Once the problem was passed on to another publisher, one that did not have a textbook division, Macmillan was accused of censoring. The conspiracists love Velikovskian imaginings; the astronomers do not and overreacted, which is incomprehensible, since they ignore astrology, haruspication, tyromancy, and hundreds of other insanities.

Gordon Moran, in *Silencing Scientists*, presents a series of cases in which scientists, as well as scholars in other fields, suppress (which for Moran is "more encompassing" than mere censorship) fellow scholars' work that they dislike. This they do by misusing peer review (4), abusing their authority (5), citing national security and threatening libel and defamation suits (7), favoring collegiality (14), and adhering to politically correct thought processes (123).

The history of censorship is a long and detailed litany of demagogues who wish to control what others read or view, and it is not necessary here to recapitulate the intellectual and physical losses to deprived individuals or cultures because of the physical destruction of the written word—at the Alexandrian Library, the pyre of Mayan codices that Diego de Landa ordered, the Serbian bombing of the Bosnian national library, and so on. This sample series of unnecessary and incinerating debacles destroyed millions of sometimes unique volumes. But similar results were obtained on a much more personal level.

---

*The Jungle, Upton Sinclair's fictional account of the meat packing industry and how inedible rubbish is passed on to the consumer improved matters. It shows precisely why government regulation and inspection are necessary in a world of uncaring and greedy capitalists. But not enough: More than half a century ago, this author watched a worker throw detritus including string into a machine making chopped meat for restaurants. No wonder weird things turn up on people's plates, a caterpillar, for example, in his spinach.

The Scope of Information Ethics

Frances Stellof* offered censorable books to her customers at the Gotham Book Mart including the works of Joyce, Miller, and others whom the authorities could not abide. She suffered greatly for her courageous fight against the pathologically controlling. *Wise Men Fish Here*, her biography, is a fascinating account of her tribulations and successes. There naturally exist hundreds of works that might bear mention; especially noteworthy is *Girls Lean Back Everywhere*, Edward DeGrazia's comprehensive overview of literary censorship and Louis Menand's fascinating *New Yorker* article covering the roles played by editors and publishers—especially Jack Kahane and Maurice Girodias in Paris and Barney Rosset† in New York—in bringing about an end to censorious control of "obscene" literary works sometimes through court cases.

Time wreaks havoc with memory but nevertheless it is astonishing to see how far we already had degenerated a quarter of a century ago when Nat Hentoff published *Free Speech for Me But Not for Thee*. If things appear abysmal today, especially in educational institutions and politics, they were not much better in 1992 when political correctness reared its ugly head on page after page: censor; control; protect everyone from themselves, *Huckleberry Finn*, pornography, sexism, racism, feminists, Nazis, and ideas, and fight for and against, and never let up. Despite the absoluteness of the first Amendment, government, in the form of school boards, for example, and other organizations and individuals abrogate it with impunity. The judicial arms of the federal and state government tender opinions, many of which contradict each other. Things are bound to get worse.

Astonishingly, Catharine MacKinnon, a constitutional scholar, advo-

---

*Steloff, a vegetarian, who came down to work when she was 100, was still feisty when the present author's wife worked for her (as did Tennessee Williams long before). The then current Gotham Book Mart owner told my wife to take Steloff to the Museum of Modern Art by cab. They left the store and my wife moved away; Steloff asked why. She said that she was going to get a cab. Steloff replied that Hauptman could take a cab but that she was walking. She was 100 years old.

†Rosset owned Grove Press which published wonderfully outlandish work. In the 1950s and 60s, the present author would wander along New York's Astor Place, "Book Row," with its ca. 50 used book emporia. Here and there one found Grove press volumes such as James Hogg's *Private Memoirs and Confessions of a Justified Sinner, The Evergreen Reader*, and perhaps works by Ionesco, Borges, or Beckett; he bought these and thereby was exposed to material that he might never have encountered elsewhere.

---

cates extensive censoring of pornography on the ground that it causes harm and this despite the fact that it would abrogate the First Amendment's protection of free speech. It is easy to sympathize with the ostensible damage (defamation, discrimination, racial and sexual harassment, inequality, physical harm) caused by sexually explicit materials—except that there is no evidence that this is the case and it would entail the abrogation of rights guaranteed by the Constitution and subsequent case law. In fact, MacKinnon's ostensibly reasonable argument is precisely why pornography should *not* be censored, which becomes clear once it is deconstructed as Tony Doyle does when he takes MacKinnon to task in a detailed critique of many of the sometimes unconvincing points she makes especially in *Only Words.* Doyle rebuts MacKinnon, who insists that pornography harms by increasing violence, exploiting the actors, perpetuating inequality, and resembling actual assault. But these opinions are not backed up by empirical evidence And anything that truly is harmful is "already against the law." Doyle concludes that "...MacKinnon fails to show that pornography harms in any of the ways that she supposes" (Doyle, "MacKinnon" 56, 57, 60, 68).

There is no doubt that pornography *might* be exploitive but the same thing can be said of slavery, capitalism, global outsourcing, and deunionization. Interestingly, there is at least a possibility that this whole business is a subconscious defense of a prudish attitude toward "deviant" sexual activity that others hold to be perfectly normal and acceptable. Never forget that many people negate dancing, nakedness, polyamory, polygamy, and polyandry. No decent human being would defend rape or violence against anyone, but these actions occur very infrequently in pornography and if and when they do, they are simulated. This is *not* the same thing as real assault, real rape, or real harm. And simulations do not necessarily lead to the real thing. (Snuff films—if they truly exist—are no different than premeditated murder and perpetrators should be imprisoned for life.) There is simply no convincing argument that textual or imagistic depictions of sexual activity should be censored or expunged.

It is necessary to repeat that much pornography is neither abusive nor violent (MacKinnon admits that "This does not presume that all pornography is made through abuse..." [20]) and it is far less painful or harmful to viewers than the vile and repugnant violence that occurs as a matter of course in serious, influential, and highly praised Hollywood films such as *Saving Private Ryan* or *Hacksaw Ridge.* Do decent people enjoy *Hunger Games,* a film that entertains by having children kill their peers? Even worse are horror films aimed at susceptible and impressionable male and female preteens and teenagers who seem to relish and enjoy them. This naturally inures them to the violence and horror that they will encounter as they grow up and take part in a world that offers real brutality, assault, rape, torture, murder, and warfare.

But most important, consider this astonishing point: Normal, upstanding men and women (ranging in age from young adults to much older grandparents) produce still images of themselves in extremely compromising positions and then mount them on the Internet or videotape themselves and mount these amateur, extremely sexually explicit films on YouTube or other sites, acts that vitiate almost everything that MacKinnon contends. This is certainly inexplicable and one might think extraordinarily embarrassing, but this does not seem to stifle an apparently ubiquitous compulsion.

Even the implications of the infamous statement by Justice Potter Stewart, that he knows hard-core pornography when he sees it, have been culturally and legally superseded. Physical and digital pornography is a thriving industry fulfilling some innate human need. Those who dislike it on religious or familial grounds continue to rail and fight against it, but it appears as if they have lost the battle. (See also Chapter 11.)

One might legitimately argue that certain types, categories, or genres of information should be delimited (censored), as the courts often have, but the results are almost always counter-productive. With the exception of truly potentially harmful information (such as personal financial or national security data or nuclear missile launch codes) information should be free, not financially, but available rather than controlled. Indeed, critics insist, and rightly so, that a high percentage of the government's confidential, secret, and top secret materials should be declassified. Statutes such as the 1996 Communications Decency Act (CDA), the 1998 Children's Online Privacy Protection Act (COPPA), and the 2000 Children's Internet Protection Act (CIPA), which, as is often the case, mean well but which essentially attempt to control readers and viewers (and especially children) from encountering sexual material, should never have been passed into law, and the courts often agreed. With few exceptions, intellectual freedom demands uncensored materials. (See also Chapter 14.)

But the esteemed scholar Amitai Etzioni disagrees: "In short, materials that directly endanger lives, [bomb making manuals] should be banned from the Internet." "...[E]ven free speech, needs to be balanced with other ... [rights], especially the right to live" (66). So, it is patently obvious to the most fervent defender of intellectual freedom, the First Amendment, and free speech that words do matter, that they sometimes cause palpable harm (for the pen *is* mightier than the sword), and that those who are slandered, libeled, defamed, offended, insulted, hated, frightened, aggrieved, or hurt should have some form of redress; and they do.

Demanding that anyone including students be stifled for mentioning an idea or theory that one finds intolerable, or disrupting a speaker articulating an irreligious or undemocratic or hateful concept, is censorious and unacceptable to those who care about the life of the mind. Instead, as this author has long contended, the expression must be allowed but any real harm that ensues can be punished locally, that is, within the confines of its genesis, whether a government agency, a business, or an academic institution. When this fails, a suit can be brought in a state or federal court. Here, naturally, the offense must be proven, which is not the case when someone accuses outside a legal environment, where petty tyrants make unjust decisions. No one would want to be under the jurisdiction of a dean who had the effrontery to tell someone that her department has too many lesbian members. As noted, censorship is anathema. Countless studies have been published on the topic as well as on book bannings and burnings. None of this, however, has stopped "European officials" from demanding that the large technology companies "curb online hate speech" and sometimes they comply (Scott "Europe").

Libraries have been in the forefront of protecting our right to read and view. (See Martha Cornog's historical overview.) There also exist many organizations that fight against censorship and advocate for those attacked. See, for example, the National Coalition Against Censorship (http://ncac.org/). See also the fall 1997 issue of the *Journal of Information Ethics* devoted to "First Amendment Rights."

11   Computer Ethics and the Internet

Computer Ethics

Computers have been an integral part of the American landscape for almost three-quarters of a century. The earliest practical devices were large mainframes that were employed in government and business. Most laypersons were unaware of their existence. They were large, primitive units with dumb terminals and did their job in batches using pre-encoded punch cards. Eventually, many corporations began to employ these devices and operators, some of whom ran their data at night. They had no direct bearing nor effect on the general public. During the 1970s, libraries began to replace their card catalogs with computers; the terminals allowed for searching the local collection and that was all. It was only in the late 1970s that personal computers began to be used in organizations and educational facilities and it was then that they began to influence the way things were done. Adventurous individuals bought these primitive units or built them from kits. They were, in fact, merely computers: They did computations and allowed for composing and drawing; they did not connect to any external sources. Libraries via librarians also had access to commercial databases that allowed for searching in hundreds of individual disciplines. These searches were sometimes amazingly expensive (hundreds or thousands of dollars) and the cost was often subsidized by the public or academic institution.

Naturally, students took advantage of this generosity and requested that one or two or ten long and detailed annual corporate reports be printed on a lethargic and noisy dot matrix printer. They then tossed these enormous documents into the trash. When the earliest avatar of the Internet arrived, many academic libraries fought against allowing their computers, which derived information from CD-Roms, to interact with the Internet, but eventually everyone capitulated, and Internet access exploded in businesses, schools, homes, and now on the road, any road, anywhere.

Computer ethics is now a well developed subdiscipline with a buckling bookshelf of excellent monographs and journal articles that attempt to lead one along the right path. For those with integrity and a well-developed moral compass, things go well. For hackers, crackers, cybercriminals such as credit card or identity thieves, things are even better— until they are caught. As is often the case, when people fail to act decently, the law steps in (in combat boots). (Cybercrime costs the world economy a great deal of money: two trillion dollars by 2019.) Kevin Mitnick, one will recall, went to prison; and in late 2016, Alonzo Knowles, who hacked the email accounts of celebrities and removed unreleased scripts and music, financial material "and nude and intimate images and videos" (see Chapter 10, contra MacKinnon) received a five year prison term (Weiser), but this is a most unusual result. Indeed, most computer criminals get away with their transgressions. As Deborah Johnson points out, Robert T. Morris, Jr., who created a very harmful worm, was charged and found guilty under the 1986 Computer Fraud and Abuse Act. He did not serve five years nor pay a $250,000 fine. Indeed, he did not go to prison at all. He was placed on probation, fined $10,000, and had to do some community service (D.G. Johnson, "Computer" 81–82). As with research misconduct miscreants, these penalties (which in this case appear to be severe) are inadequate to deter hacking, cracking, theft, and other horrors.

As with most professional and even occupational areas, the lay public has only the most superficial practical knowledge, that which allows it to function. For example, many people know how a circuit breaker works and some can change one, but they would have a harder time installing a receptacle especially if they know nothing about live, neutral, and ground wiring. It would be almost impossible for them to competently and safely wire a new dwelling. They understand that a will is a necessity but without aid of some kind they might make a crucial error. And so on through almost everything one might consider. And so it is with computers. Users learn precisely what they need to know but no more. They have other things to do, naturally. If they do not require the use of reader audio output created for the visually impaired, they will not know it exists, let alone how to install and use it.

This business is most salient when it comes to protecting systems from incursions. Users have heard of trojan horses, worms, viruses, and software that protects, but rogue anti-virus is a mystery. And they manifest skepticism or forgetfulness when given suggestions on how to avoid imminent catastrophe. They do not back up; they do not use adequate protections such as fire walls; but they do click on alien links in emails from scammers; they do respond to Nigerian princes who have lots of money to give them; they do use common wireless access at airports; they do leave their laptops, filled with top secret data, in their cars; they do unethically share commercial passwords (so that Sci-Hub can steal); and they create passwords like 123 456 or ones based on their puppies' names or their birthdays.

Computing and Internet interactions are now taken for granted in the same way that plumbing is. Most people never give these things any thought until they go away for a few days only to discover that a tiny pipe connector on the toilet has disintegrated and the entire house is overflowing with water. (This did happen to someone.) Subsequently, they might turn off the main water supply when going away for an extended period. But probably not: Very few people take extreme precautions. This author once visited the home of a well-known person who went abroad for six months. He and his wife left their refrigerator full of food. Although my visit occurred 40 years ago, I have a vivid image of the rotting foodstuffs.

In 1985, Deborah Johnson produced the first major study of computer ethics. Many others, including textbooks for aspiring computer scientists, followed. They address problems logically associated with computers and the procedures that these devices allow. The term must now encompass not merely desk- and laptop versions, but also tablets, smart phones and watches, as well as any forthcoming apparatus that allows access to external cyberspace. Ethical incursions are not limited to connectivity, though. A non-networked computer can, for example, turn out fabricated documents (as early Canon copiers could duplicate money).

In management, banking, and business in general, many opportunities exist to act unethically. (In fact, business as well as politics are two major areas in which there is a real disinclination to nurture ethical commitment over personal gain: Greed, corruption, and malfeasance are common occurrences.) A famous example, is the siphoning of mere pennies to an external bank account; these tiny amounts from millions of people add up to a tidy profit for the embezzler. (See also Chapter 15.) Ethical incursions in cyberspace range from copyright infringement, piracy, and theft to cracking and trolling. As noted, computer ethics (which, in the early days, some scholars disparaged as not necessary, since conventional ethics covered its territory), is merely a subset of IE. Indeed, in 2001, in the third edition of her *Computer Ethics*, Johnson mentions that she thought about changing the title to "Information Ethics" (xv). Many of its concerns which also include, as Smith observes, "expert systems, artificial intelligence, and robotics" (Smith, M.M. 340), are either ignored or discussed in various chapters of this book.

Johnson ascribes many of the ethical problems to "policy vacuums" (6), that is, one does not have a solid understanding of what should be done in a specific situation especially when the applications are new. She insists that the "traditionalist account" is inadequate, incapable of solving the new and complex challenges associated with computers (8). The present author has long insisted that new technologies do not require a new ethic nor a revised approach to making ethical decisions. There is no doubt that unique situations arise in cyberspace, and that they may require a revised way of looking at and understanding them as they relate to individuals and society, but they always reflect some aspect of reality. The application of deontological or consequentialist thinking or a combination of both modalities would allow one to reach a viable decision in both realms.

This does not deny the very different types of challenges that exist when computers are engaged. And naturally, ethical dilemmas are sometimes irresolvable. But computer infractions are susceptible to the human ethic that has developed over many millennia and the means of reaching decisions that have evolved in the Western world. Anything that replaces rather than augments what is already in place must be truly spectacular. Johnson does a fair and judicious job of presenting her case including precise problems such as the ethicality of cookies, data mining, and image manipulation (6–7), but as far as this author can tell, she does not offer a viable alternative to the traditionalist account; in fact, she does not seem to present an alternative at all.

If there is a bottom line here, it is that computers, systems, networks, and applications should never disenfranchise, dehumanize, or diminish the integrity of the person. Each human being is unique, has inherent worth, and is as different from a silicon controlled mechanism (no matter how effective it may appear to be) as a raindrop is from the Nile (see Chapter 18). There is a point at which comparisons and connections cease to have any meaning. And it is here too that one must note that Simon Head is correct: Reliance on "smarter machines" is turning us into fools: Computer business systems (CBSs) control, micromanage, diminish earnings through deskilling, objectify, and dehumanize us (3, 12, 27).

The Internet

It is very easy to be seduced, so that IE is confused with the ethical use of technology. This is the source of the excellent journal *Ethics and Information Technology*, but there are obviously many more problems associated with informational etiology and application than those that arise from technological advancements. Nevertheless, and to partially counter what is presented above, when the delimited Arpanet gave birth to the ubiquitous Internet, it created a plethora of ethical complications, some of which appear to be unresolvable. This does seem to be very different from the ethical breaches associated with un-networked computers, where traditional ethical mandates may be able to solve much simpler problems. The Internet creates clashes between, for example, freedom of speech and libel or privacy and communication, that differ from the same conflicts when they occur outside of cyberspace; no international judicial or policing force exists to control matters in a world consisting of digital bits and bytes; although governments could control, censor, suppress, or shut down sites, they generally do not, even when extreme criminal harm such as hate, trolling, and financial scams result. This is a legacy of net neutrality.

The Internet is a boon to those who wish to discover, learn, communicate, or promulgate. Much of what one can locate is superb in every way; some is problematic; far too much is propagandistic or false (sites exist that publish exclusively fake news [Manjoo B7] and a film company created "fake news sites" to lure people to *A Cure for Wellness* [Stack B1]); some is illegal or criminal; and some is harmful, vilely repugnant, hateful, terroristic, in a word, evil. Cyberethics ostensibly provides guidance for correct action. It fails and failed miserably (as did other deterrents) during the 2016 presidential election when Russian hackers broke into American systems and sabotaged the results. No one should confuse foreign interference and subversion in domestic governance with political machinations; it matters little which political party is responsible (if any) and which benefits. It is probable that this sabotage altered the course of American history. America is not a Third World demagogic monarchy; this should not happen here and the government (and the political parties) should do a much better job of protecting themselves from cyber-intrusion. We are almost one-fifth of the way through the 21st century. It should be possible to emplace an electronic wall that is impregnable to hackers. If not, no sane, responsible person should post critical materials online. The convenience is countered by the debacles, as people constantly note but do not learn to avoid.

Richard Spinello first published *Cyberethics* in 2002; the fifth revised edition presents an excellent and lucid overview of philosophical underpinnings and the problems that they may help to solve through regulation. To the two main sources of control (norms, i.e., ethics, and law) explored in the present study, Spinello adds Lawrence Lessig's market and code (2–3). The former is not all that positively effective and the latter manages to elicit personal data (through cookies, for example) and allows hackers to infiltrate; it also does a poor job of protecting users from pop-up advertisements, spam, fake news, worms, viruses, and other injurious infusions. In email systems, it filters legitimate and important documents and sends them to clutter, spam, or junk files. The market is undependable and code injurious.

Social media provides a platform for people to share information, thoughts, photographic images, and reciprocal debates. But Twitter's tweetings often degenerate into nasty if succinct altercations, severe threats, and other ugly, stress-inducing jibes that sometimes result from an innocent remark. The dangers inherent in this public communication, on Facebook and Twitter, for example, may not be worth the risk of emotional or even physical harm; this type of nasty interaction occurs more often in the Internet underworld. And celebrities especially enjoy harassing each other, even if they are related. Cyber-bullying takes many forms including secret recordings (illegal in some venues), sexual humiliation, revenge pornography, and "mob deployment." These nasty feuds have included Kanye West and Taylor Swift as well as Rob Kardashian and Kylie Jenner (Hess).

Serious hurtful trolling occurs in the Internet's subbasement, a place that only a limited number of the world's enormous online population visits. (Many terms are used to demarcate this area, where material is difficult to locate: splinternet, invisible Web, dark Web, deep Internet, or hidden Web [Sarokin 157]). But Facebook and other media cannot entirely avoid the negative outbursts that sully human communication. Twitter, for example, is home to anonymous posters who rail against anyone they dislike and angry, abusive, harassing, racist, sexist, misogynistic hate speech fills the Twittersphere.*

It is often difficult to stifle or ban the posters for many reasons, especially the fear of censorship accusations. Political and personal commitment bring out the worst in these adults, but even children can blast their own friends and acquaintances with vicious and vulgar bile and rancor.†

Both adults and youngsters enjoy calling each other names: "You are a despicable whore"; "You deserve all those death threats you are getting"; "Shut the fuck up bitch...." These articulate correspondents, with extensive

---

*It is astonishing, indeed incomprehensible, that here we have the free flow of the vilest rubbish ever articulated in a public forum, and some of the same people who utter this tripe are, undoubtedly, high school and college students who demand trigger warnings, safe spaces, and protection from anything that might upset them. I wonder if they study war, the Holocaust, and epidemics, watch the nightly news featuring horrific reports and images of bombed cities, and damaged human beings—in Viet Nam, Iraq, Chad, Sudan, Syria, and even the United States, where the World Trade Center, the Boston Marathon, and other atrocities were (gleefully) featured by the major networks as well as in Hollywood cinema. (See Chapter 14 for extensive elaboration.)

†I am indebted here to my daughter who from the age of nine until 15 (at the time of this writing) has interacted in some way on Snapchat, Vine, Instagram, Facebook, YouTube, and Twitter and has apprised me of the sometimes hateful ripostes that take place between and among preteens, adolescents, and teenagers.

vocabularies, are familiar with and very fond of terms for the procreative act or female body parts.

When not wasting time texting, posting, or hurling invective and threats, a surprising number of people enjoy the sexual pleasures that the Internet proffers. Each year billions of searches are done and billions of dollars spent on online pornographic materials, despite the fact that much of it is free. Easily accessible sexually oriented books, magazines, and films have existed at least since 1953 when *Playboy* first appeared.* This author's brother had a subscription when he was still an adolescent, and R- and X-rated films played in theaters. But the Internet makes available extreme material in extraordinary abundance to anyone with access. For many adults, this is probably not a pressing problem, but for those offended for personal, social, or religious reasons and for young children, it is an ideological, cultural, and social nightmare. But it constitutes what Marty Klein terms "PornPanic," yet another misguided moral panic concerning sexuality, "artificial threats inflated by the media and public figures"; he points out that as Internet pornography has increased, "rape, divorce, suicide, and child sexual exploitation have all *decreased...*" (23, 26).

Some family members pledge not to view such material in any venue. The plague that even comic books foisted upon our youth, as outlined in Fredric Wertham's classic 1954 *Seduction of the Innocent,* and censored (literary) obscenity, fully discussed in the Kronhausens' seminal 1959 *Pornography and the Law (*and bizarrely confirmed by the regressive 1986 *Meese Report),* have been fully countered, as obscene material is now readily available. For example, "XVideos is the fifty-sixth most popular Web site in the world" and "in 2014, Pornhub ... had seventy-eight billion page views..." (Forrester 64). People watch a lot of pornography (and amateurs make it too).

Cybercrime is ubiquitous in cyberspace. It is not necessary to leave the real world to lose one's identity, but the Internet helps and facilitates ID transfers. ATMs, online banking and purchasing, and the revelation of data to scammers can easily result in ID loss, which in turn will result in the loss of money; this may remain hidden for years: A thief can open an

---

*Prior to this, the U.S. post office confiscated copies of *Ulysses* (which it burned), *Lady Chatterley's Lover,* and many other classics. (See Chapter 10 for a detailed discussion.)

account in a person's name, charge expenses and purchases to it, pay the low monthly fee, and continue to use the fraudulent credit card with impunity. Terrorism, which affects society as well as individuals, is fomented and facilitated by the Internet, which spreads the word across the globe. P. N. Grabosky and Russell G. Smith delineate and discuss a host of digital crimes including theft of services; criminal communication; piracy, counterfeiting, and forgery; offensive material; extortion; money laundering and tax evasion; and vandalism and terrorism. Stolen data such as that lost by Yahoo is sold on the dark web. There is more but I think that that is enough.

Facebook, Twitter, and many other social media sites provide the vast majority of innocent people with a means to communicate personal experiences, messages, opinions, and images. But they can be abused, sometimes horrifically: Trolling and cyberbullying attacks can be so vilely oppressive that people remove themselves from cyberspace; sometimes they commit suicide.

Charles Ess distinguishes between analogue and digital media (10) and resuscitates the question that has been posed for half a century (and one we have recently encountered): Is a new ethic for digital media necessary? As usual, the present author demurs; everything is in place to handle the most pressing ethical problems in the digital environment. Ess offers immediate smartphone photography and posting as an example (13) of a more responsible— ... what? how does this differ from a 1950s paparazzo who clicked and published embarrassing images in *The National Enquirer?* That it is easier and quicker to post (15) and easier to alter others' texts or images (17) does not require a new ethic or even a new way of making ethical decisions; in all of Ess's cases (and any other he might devise), a respectful, considerate, and caring attitude would go a long way to making an ethical decision (if one were even necessary). When true dilemmas present themselves, Kant and Mill can help even the confused and perplexed. And, of course, sometimes, no tenable solution is possible.

Additionally, Ess advocates a non–Western shared or distributed responsibility for actions across networks (21). Many Western scholars become enamored of Eastern religions, especially Buddhism, which turns up here with some frequency. Confucian, Buddhist, and African philosophies that advocate shared responsibility for ethical actions are a poor paradigm for a contemporary world in which Western technologies, beliefs, and values are replacing ancient Eastern modalities. Although many people are responsible for a functioning Internet and its digital media, only the photographer or the poster or the hacker or the cyberbully is guilty of harming and it is he or she who must bear responsibility and be punished. Distributed morality is a very bad idea, one that allows individuals to shirk their ethical and legal commitments. Do we really want to embrace the time-honored, Eastern horror of punishing the relatives of criminals?

12 Privacy,
Security, Surveillance

"In public opinion surveys, Americans always favor privacy. Then they turn around and sell it cheaply. Most vehemently oppose any suggestion of a national identification system yet volunteer their telephone numbers and mother's maiden names and even—grudgingly or not—Social Security numbers...."—James Gleick

Scholars, jurists, and activist-founded organizations began to take an interest in privacy, security, and surveillance at a presciently early stage in their development: Bentham and his Panopticon in the late 18th century; Brandeis and Warren followed; Alan Westin's influential, full length study of privacy and freedom; and Gary Marx and his detailed article long before these topics demanded ongoing attention. And then the floodgates opened and legislation, books, Websites, blogs, commentary, and physical control flooded the world and continue to pour forth.

When one drove on the autobahn almost 60 years ago, or later arrived in Hong Kong, it was no real surprise to have officials point sub-machine guns at or near one (though nevertheless quite disconcerting). It *was* a disappointing and terrifying experience to arrive at an American airport shortly after the destruction of the World Trade Center (near which this author grew up 75 years ago) and be met by multiple pairs of armed soldiers (who in the United States, unlike in most other countries, have no jurisdiction over civilians) parading around intimidating the thousands of innocent travelers who were under enough stress and duress without additionally fearing an immediate attack by either a terrorist or a solder run amok.

---

12. Privacy, Security, Surveillance

Information applied ethically and judiciously is probably the single most crucial and decisive element in balancing freedom and vigilance. David Sarokin and Jay Schulkin observe that "Oddly enough, the multi-faceted tension between surveillance and privacy, security and freedom, secrecy and transparency, leaks and legitimacy, and trust and mistrust comes at a time when both government and corporations probably practice—in the Unites States, at least—a greater degree of openness than ever before" (179).

Privacy

Americans value privacy, though they favor free expression. The intellectual clash that this produces is difficult to accommodate. In Europe, privacy takes precedence; here, it is sacrificed on the altar of material purchases, gaming, social media offerings, and to a lesser extent, and theoretically, intellectual freedom and free speech. We want to protect our private musings, affairs, finances, and children from prying eyes but we offer all of this and more to companies that seduce us into buying, using store cards, and revealing personal secrets, including potentially harmful social security numbers, in exchange for virtually nothing. And we reveal our deepest secrets and real personalities in repulsive exchanges on social media. Then we get upset because the government asks us to answer some innocent census questions.

Modern American legal privacy protection traces its beginnings back to Samuel D. Warren and Louis D. Brandeis's famous 1890 article, "The Right to Privacy," published in the *Harvard Law Review.* Here the authors claim that we have "the right to be let alone" (193). They advert to gossip, slander, and libel and sustain the view that "the common law recognizes and upholds a principle applicable to cases of invasion of privacy" insofar as we communicate to others only what we wish to (196, 197, 198). They continue, "If, then, the decisions indicate a general right to privacy for thoughts, emotions, and sensations, these should receive the same protection, whether expressed in writing, or in conduct, in conversation, in attitudes, or in facial expression" (206). And this leads to, "The principle which protects personal writings and any other productions of the intellect or of the emotions, is the right to privacy, and the law has no new principle to formulate when it extends this protection to the personal appearance, sayings, acts, and to personal relation, domestic or otherwise" (213). This contracted sequence eliminates a great deal of extraneous discussion, but nevertheless the whole business is not all that convincing, and citing "common law" or previous cases does not lead to a *right* to privacy, although it may enhance it. Rights are proscribed as one may see in Chapter 13.

As the decades rolled by, privacy became ever more desirable, socially and legally, that is, laws were passed without recourse to previous foundational structures, until the government (and not just in the United States) decided it needed to protect us. Then competing legal mandates came along. The 2001 USA Patriot Act's privacy abrogations expired in 2015, but there are still many others. Still, privacy is protected by a diversity (call it a farrago) of laws including the 1986 Electronic Communications Privacy Act, the 1974 Family and Educational Privacy Act, the 1994 Driver's Privacy Protection Act, and many others. In 2001, we were burdened with the Health Insurance Portability and Accountability Act (HIPAA), which does offer some real informational protection to patients, but which also insinuates another annoying layer of bureaucracy into medical care, creates more forms to read and sign, and controls patients' access.

So, legal protection offers judicial recourse from incursions, but we also now have a social and cultural expectation of protecting personal intellectual, and physical space and this despite the insanity of social media, where people advertise the very things they would, under normal conditions, wish to conceal. It is unethical to reveal data and information that can cause harm to others. Often this is inadvertent but even more often purposeful in order to acquire or subscribe or seek revenge or cause harm. It is very difficult to counter the tide of bureaucrats who line up in order to demand one's private data. Who thinks twice about such matters? How can a public utility send one a bill without identifying data? And how can DIRECTV deal with a customer without a social security number? This author has fought back against this barrage for a quarter of a century. He refused to give data to the Immigration and Naturalization Service (now U.S. Citizenship and Immigration Services, a part of Homeland Security) and the FBI. He succeeded.

12. Privacy, Security, Surveillance

But this may not matter because *they* know where we live: In June 2004, *reason's* 40,000 subscribers each received their issue with a customized cover showing a photograph of their neighborhood and home. This must have entailed a great deal of extra work for *reason's* editors, but it was worth it: It must have horrified the subscribers. It still horrifies those who care about privacy protection.

Ess holds that the global sway of new digital media is controlled by cultural determinants (Chapter 2), which naturally vary across both time and space. But, nonetheless, he admits that despite the enormous legal differences that exist, for example, between EU and U.S. privacy policy (the philosophical differences are much smaller), a global shift is occurring so that in many Eastern countries, there is a trend away from group privacy and toward individual protections (67); and how can it be otherwise, when the Internet broadcasts everything one requires to steal someone's money, identity, and soul?

Perhaps if global communication were merely a dream, Confucian and Buddhist attitudes toward privacy would still obtain, but they are now a mere remnant of a distant past, and even mentioning them appears to be a fruitless exercise in historical speculation. To cite Buddhist (or similar Confucian or African) dogma to the effect that individual privacy is unwarranted or even unacceptable, and the abrogation (abnegation) of desire and the self is a worthy goal* (63–64), confuses religious and secular necessities and fails to accommodate the new reality, which is the very point of Ess's study, viz., that the world has changed and no Japanese Buddhist or Chinese Confucian wants his or her personal data and information broadcast to the government, cyberbullies, stalkers, or thieves. All of this is despite the high percentage of people who *do* voluntarily broadcast their most intimate data, desires, secrets, and sexually explicit images to the social media world.

Well, people are often inexplicable fools, which does not alter a general global desire to protect oneself and one's privacy in the face of cultural

---

*The Buddhist theological doctrine that calls for the abrogation of desire is not fulfilled in the practical necessity of living in the real world, where a lama in Myanmar called for the murder of Muslims and the Sherpas who help to guide mountaineers in the Himalaya desire food, drink, free Western mountaineering clothing and equipment, and excellent remuneration for their appallingly dangerous work.

pressure to post personal material and a corporate and governmental monitoring and surveillance that ambushes us in public but also in our most personal environments. Does Ess realize that taxicabs in Beijing are equipped with microphones? Do Chinese businessmen or government employees discussing proprietary or classified information wish to share this with their Confucian community cohort? Referring to the ancient dictates of Eastern religions is inordinately misleading.

Helen Nissenbaum sees things quite differently. She disagrees that it is necessary to defend against technologically enhanced privacy encroachment by "limiting access to personal information." She insists that people are not concerned with the restriction of information but rather they want it to "flow *appropriately*" and this can be accomplished through "contextual integrity" (1–2). (The right to be forgotten might give her pause; see Chapter 13.) It is possible that some people feel this way, but most do not give privacy protection much thought. They do not want to be harmed but they nevertheless wish to enjoy the convenience of ATMs and electronic payment as well as the pleasure of social media revelations not to mention public sexual display.

Nevertheless, Nissenbaum presents an excellent analysis of various aspects of privacy in terms of her contextual integrity whose (justificatory) framework consists of explanation, evaluation, and prescription (190). The goal is to understand why people react as they do and to create helpful norms (11). Among many other insightful benefits, she presents an overview of monitoring systems (Part I) and discusses Jeroen van den Hoven's reasons for privacy protection that guard against informational harm, inequality, and injustice and "encroachment on moral autonomy" (78–81). What is interesting is that the man and woman on the street do not require an admittedly superb but esoteric framework to know practically and intuitively that privacy is worth protecting, for innumerable reasons, although they often purposely fail to do so.

Many organizations offer help and protection from those who would invade our privacy, broadcast our sins, and steal our identities, including our government and criminals. Similarly to the American Civil Liberties Union (https://www.aclu.org/), the Electronic Frontier Foundation (https://www.eff.org/) does an excellent job of "defending civil liberties in the digital world" and of alerting us and guarding against the agencies that attempt to steal data without a warrant and threaten those who might indicate they had been visited by secret agents (as if this was a Conradian novel). The Electronic Privacy Information Center (https://epic.org/) does similar work protecting us from our protectors. See also the Privacy Rights Clearinghouse (www.privacyrights.org) for an enormous amount of useful information. *CIRE Current Issues in Research Ethics* is an extraordinarily valuable resource for privacy and confidentiality ("Privacy").

Security

Even if we did not live in an age of terror, when people are wantonly murdered every day through concerted efforts by individuals and groups, most of us would want and expect our governments to protect us. Indeed, this is the primary purpose of government—to safeguard its citizens. It does a really bad job. When Iran arrests or kidnaps Americans, the United States does little or nothing. It forgets to walk softly and carry a big stick. (Consider also the Philippines.) Contraveningly, the government is always intruding into other countries' business, allowing manufacturers to sell ordnance and other military paraphernalia to "allies," maintaining military bases all over the world, and sending destroyers and battleships to various locations to intimidate the intimidators. Security on- and offline depends on many things that detract from our privacy.

Our security necessitates a military presence but also the protection of intelligence. In this we (as most countries) fail even at a time when encryption and hardware should be foolproof. It is not, as hacks and cracks constantly show. And human foibles have really bad global results. Is there a knowledgeable person anywhere who does not know that his or her government is guilty, more or less, of harm, corruption, and crime? Revelations can be more damaging than maintaining silence. It is for this reason that the work of Manning and Snowdon do not deserve praise. They both were government employees; they both revealed secrets indiscriminately; and they both committed treason, although many people incorrectly think that they are whistleblowing heroes. And it is not certain that WikiLeaks is a valuable asset. Its revelations may do some good but innocent bystanders may also suffer. If the NSA, FBI, and its sister agencies hired patriotic, full-time employees rather than contractors and did not assign

---

low-level military volunteers to deal with top secret information, things would have a better outcome. Here we are dealing with informational rather than physical security, but they are intimately related, since there can be no harm or attacks or terrorism without prior information; even if individuals are acting alone, they must know what they are doing, what they require, where and when they are going, and so on. Little can be accomplished without accurate data and information. Disseminating it for harmful purposes is unethical and often illegal.

We desire to be physically secure in our persons, home, and environment. The most primitive hominid, hundreds of thousands years ago, desired a secure habitat from predators; even animals require security. Modern life has, in most cases increased security from weather incursions, warmongers, criminals, and tigers or polar bears, although these detriments sometimes overcome our defenses. The Internet has altered the security landscape and created vulnerabilities never before imagined. Cybersecurity for individuals, corporations, public utilities, and government agencies, particularly the military, is perhaps the single most pressing issue that we face. Hacking and cracking can cause irremediable damage. Cybercrime cost the world (circa 2015) more than 400 million dollars derived from the two to three trillion dollars spent on the Internet (Lucas 16, 17). And of course it is not just crazed teenagers who enjoy and profit from their online madness; governments including our own surveil, steal from, and sabotage other governments' sites. Herman Tavani suggests a three-pronged defense that covers data, systems, and networks (172). And four obvious solutions present themselves: Back up data and information in a diversity of modes; protect systems technologically; control access absolutely; do not share critical data or control over a publicly accessible network. These are all so simple that a child could implement any or all of them.

Here, as with intellectual freedom and democracy, as noted above, we depend upon ethical commitment (moral suasion) rather than legal control, but often neither has any effect. Nevertheless, we continue to pass germane laws, lots of them, some of which protect individuals, especially children, from themselves, but others originate from the desire to protect computers and their data, e.g., the Computer Security Act of 1987 protects government information.

------

12. Privacy, Security, Surveillance

A more secure nation can be ensured by a more secretive government (and a more repressive, totalitarian one as well), at least that is what some bureaucrats seem to think. And many of those secrets can be derived from scrupulously surveilling everyone at all times. Philip Doty analyzes this conjunction of abominations in terms of risk management in a long and detailed overview that concludes that secrecy can actually threaten security (36) and we require a new means of defending ourselves other than risk management and the "war on terror": Secrecy and surveillance are counterproductive and harmful (37).

Surveillance

More than 50 years ago, we transitioned into the information age. And now we have reaped our inheritance: the information society is susceptible to ubiquitous surveillance. In 1998, Gary Marx, preceded by Michel Foucault *inter alia,* presciently noted that ethics must adjust to the new surveillance, which he describes in a lengthy article that presents extensive principles that can encompass "all forms of technological personal data collection and use, not just those involving computers" (Marx "Ethics" 172). Almost 20 years later, he developed his ideas and brought them together in *Windows into the Soul,* an all-encompassing discussion of surveillance which here has a far more wide-ranging meaning than the word normally implies. The "watchers" scrutinize, rather than merely observe, in obvious as well as obscure ways (Marx, *Windows* passim*).* Early and inefficient monitoring in business has evolved along with dependence on computerization but large American post offices were equipped with hanging viewing walkways more than half a century ago. From high up hidden observers could watch workers through little slots (even in male and female bathrooms) to make sure nothing was stolen.*

---

*It is sad to report that this system was rather ineffective. One day, in the mid–1960s, at a large post office in New York City, this author witnessed a young employee throwing a one pound sample bag of Gold Medal flour up in the air. It came down and passed through his hands and exploded on the floor. He scooped up the powder along with the filth and detritus that litter postal floors and sent the cloth bag on its way. He was never reprimanded either because the act was not observed by a supervisor or because the surveilling overseers did not care about such foolishness.

The Scope of Information Ethics

Marx points out that surveillance attempts to control, discover, protect, verify, and sell, among other possibilities (65). In addition to what most people consider to be surveillant activity we have scrutiny of our biological persons and within the general culture (in music and art). Surveillance, both the old (accomplished through the "unaided senses") (17) and the new (managed through technical means) (20) can be attacked and this various organizations and individuals do attempt to accomplish by avoiding, distorting, blocking, and refusing through the application of technologies, norms, and contraction (145 and passim).

Surveillance cameras, drones, satellites and one's next door neighbor are watching, waiting to pounce when something goes wrong. One is fingerprinted, scanned, genetically analyzed, denied, arrested, and prosecuted (based on unreliable tests). The interesting thing is that the innocent man or woman on the street is recorded and blithely goes about his or her business; the criminal knows someone is watching but nevertheless holds up the bank, is traced, tracked, and caught. He does not seem to care. The Internet of things connects personal security cameras, protection systems, and medical records, so that one's Tuscaloosa front door can be locked or unlocked from Darjeeling—by the tenant as well as anyone else. Interior home monitoring devices can be hacked so that mother, father, and baby are visible to marauding, tech-savvy criminals. And, naturally, anyone can peer into the smart refrigerator and see the marijuana brownies on the bottom shelf.

Why do people fall for this garbage? And then there are police body cameras that indicate what is occurring. This may prove that an officer is or is not acting justly. Someone wins, but someone also loses. And does anyone consider the invaded privacy of the innocent bystander, victim, or criminal? Things continue to worsen: Facial recognition systems include many millions of visages, control Americans (many of them black), and are abused by law enforcement. The fear is that their use will "stifle free speech" and attempt to regulate politics, religion, and race. A warrant should be required to implement them (Victor).

In *Missed Information*, Sarokin and Schulkin include a four page chart that lays out some of the "mass surveillance" programs instigated by the government. The NSA, British intelligence, the post office, FBI, and others monitor calls, e- and regular mail, Webcam images, license plates, banking, and more. And millions, billions of records are involved (180–183). The number, breadth, coverage, and scope of these invasions are truly stunning. One wonders whether anyone ever scrupulously considers the true effectiveness of all of this probing. This type of secretive observation of citizens, which encroaches on Constitutionally protected freedoms, may occasionally reveal something that does involve a real threat or horror, but since observational spying can only bear fruit when someone communicates in some way—by speaking or mailing or purchasing—when a terrorist, for example, works alone, all of this scrutiny yields nothing.

To some degree, this is why the World Trade Center and many lives were destroyed and why the Cole, and Paris, and other locations have suffered damage and death. But placing an emphasis on governmental oversight may result in ignoring or taking for granted commercial monitoring, for which we are responsible—by online purchasing, communicating, sharing, and viewing. Timothy Wu is adamant that the resultant secretive acquisition of information "is a more thoroughly invasive effort than any N.S.A. data collection ever disclosed" (Senior). Like many other hateful or harmful things, we have come to take this for granted as a small price to pay for Internet pleasure and convenience, which falls precisely under "the ethic of convenience," a concept this author elucidated in 1983 (Hauptman "Ethics").

Torin Monahan discusses technologies that control through deceptive practices. Examples include Volkswagen's software that fooled the devices testing for pollution, deceptive hotel thermostats that indicate whether a room is occupied and can control lighting and temperature (230, 232), and business spyware that records what employees are doing (233). Deceptive systems are normal technologies: "They are polyvalent and polyvocal; they are oriented toward surveillance and control, especially in their hidden functions; and they are commonplace and often legal" (237). The point here is that it can be legal to deceive, spy, and control, but from any human point of view and from the perspective of the victims, this is all highly unethical. Here is where the clash between ethics and the law becomes most salient. And since the law allows such activity, it thrives, because ethical commitment is transitory.

None of this deters Holman W. Jenkins, Jr., a *Wall Street Journal* columnist, from letting us know that "surveillance *is* the answer" to terrorism.

We can surveil "without turning a nation into a police state" and this can be accomplished using big-data surveillance. All of our informational footprints could result in a total information awareness scheme, but most people who use Google, Amazon, email, or EZ-Pass are innocently searching for Godot and *Pride and Prejudice*, writing to their elderly in-laws, or trying to reach Brooklyn. They are not engaged in bombing plots, which are not so blatantly advertised. One hopes that Jenkins is correct, but he fears he is wrong.

All of the current probing misery can be traced back historically to four major events. The first is Bentham's proposal for his panoptical prison, an improvement on the repugnant systems used not only in the distant past in England and on Devil's Island, but also in France in the mid-twentieth century (an incarceration so barbaric that I hesitate to describe it). But the Panopticon's potential omnipresent surveillance is equally horrendous. The second influence was Foucault's *Discipline and Punish*, which takes all overseers to task, but also helped to disseminate panopticism. Next, we have both governmental and business desires to know everything about everyone, and England was in the forefront here, installing hundreds of cameras in London. And finally, in the United States, this was more extremely necessitated by the attack on the World Trade Center compounded by all other acts of global terrorism. Surveillance is now unavoidable and privacy is an impossible dream, although Marx holds that surveillance is a neutral activity dependent on context (*Windows* 284) and that we are not losing the battle against it (*Windows* 293–296). (See the spring 2017 issue of the *Journal of Information Ethics* for some incisive papers on Bentham's ideas [Duff "Contra"; Tylor]; *Surveillance & Society* with dedicated issues on performance [Taylor Swift and Miley Cyrus!], big data, sport, children, and so on; the summer 2005 issue of *Social Text*, entirely devoted to surveillance; and the December 2005 number of *Ethics and Information Technology* covering "Surveillance and Privacy.")

13 Law

Ethics controls through personal, social, or moral suasion, all of which may derive from a higher power such as religious or familial acculturation, fear, or simply the desire to do what one believes to be the good or right action. Legal mandates necessitate adherence because breaking the law has unpleasant consequences including fines, imprisonment, and a personal record that one carries along forever. Even a minor infraction is cause for concern; a felony or federal imprisonment can alter one's career and life, since many penalties accrue, not the least of which is that one may be unemployable, denied the right to vote, and socially ostracized. In the case of certain crimes—murder, kidnapping, rape, and especially sex offenses and pedophilia—one may be barred locally or federally from living in a specific location or be branded, so that neighbors know that the perpetrator has committed a horrible crime. At times, the heinous quality of the offense is more severe for some observers than for others. For example, a man convicted of second degree murder, who has served his time, may be far less disliked or feared than a person caught with child pornography on his cell phone, who tries to move to a suburban neighborhood with many little children.

The law has many roles to play within an informational context. Naturally, if people treated each other with respect and did not abandon considerate informational norms in areas such as privacy, defamation, cyberbullying, or advertising, there would be little need for legal sanctions. But very bright people can be simultaneously inconsiderate, greedy, and stupid. Even now, more than half a century later, it seems impossible that Edmund Wilson, an egotistical bully (who once lost his temper because a new, young *New Yorker* editor *changed a comma* in his submission), would publicly criticize Vladimir Nabokov's translation of *Eugene Onegin*. He obviously failed to consider how his friend would react and the consequences of this informational breach, especially since Nabokov was equally egomaniacal.

As is often the case, the severest penalties are for theft (rather than, say, assault). Many films on cassettes or disks for which one has paid a fair price begin with a warning that copying will result in a $50,000 fine. This is extremely unreasonable, but it is the type of legislation promulgated by entertainment companies' lobbyists* who convince legislators to sympathize with the corporate elite and their legal counsel, rather than the man or child on the street. One should not steal film by making copies, but one should also not steal bread or skirts or tires or construction material. Here the potential penalties are rather less harsh. (When a famous celebrity is caught shoplifting, she probably gets off with a slap on the wrist.)

The law impinges on informational issues in many ways and venues, though this differs dramatically from country to country. In the United States, one may speak as one wishes, though political correctness stifles communication and often results in self-censorship (see Chapter 10). In Germany, it is illegal to deny the Holocaust. In China, the law may prohibit piracy, but it cannot be too punitive, since people create vast troves of new movies and sell them to those who care little for either the law or the ethical life. In the United States, the news media strive for truth, although the Trumpian government creates its own reality. In Russia, there is no legal penalty for officially promulgating falsity, as *Pravda* and the state often do.

---

*Lobbying is an unsavory business. Individuals who desire change or require redress through Congress cannot afford to hire a lobbyist. According to the Constitution, it should be possible for any citizen to "address" Congress and we do do that through our calls or letters to senators and representatives. But this minor attempt at persuasion is a far cry from the lobbying efforts of large corporations that represent their own financial interests and persuade legislators to make sweeping changes by employing, as AT&T does, almost 100 lobbyists (and also making enormous monetary contributions to lawmakers). There exists here an egregious set of conflicts of interests. Lobbying is unethical; it should be illegal.

Warrants

The twentieth century's severe turn to terrorism has resulted in governmental protection sometimes carried to an extreme. No one wants to be harmed, maimed, or killed; no wants others to suffer these same fates; and no one wants their property to be destroyed. So it is easy to sympathize with our elected officials' desire to implement new and more draconian ways of protecting the country, its citizens, and their possessions. But sometimes, the means are so extreme that the vitiation or abolition of our basic civil liberties are not acceptable. Where one stands on this issue is dependent on the particular individual's perspective and it is probable that a person will fluctuate between the two positions desiring safety but also not wanting to lose Constitutional rights; once the Constitution is abrogated, it takes a long time and a great deal of work to restore rights that were taken for granted for decades or centuries.

Intelligence agencies use many methods to forestall terrorist attacks, including spying, listening in on phone conversations, and controlling how the innocent communicate. Somehow, agencies such the NSA, FBI, and CIA are able to convince judges to issue warrants that disallow individuals or organizations from indicating that they have been queried or controlled. After the World Trade Center bombing, librarians, for example, were questioned about suspects who used library computers. They were then prohibited from mentioning this to the media. It is ironic that when librarians came forth on their own and indicated that some suspects had used computers, they were criticized by peers for breaching patron confidentiality. The protection of information seekers' privacy is a beneficial core value of the information professions (analogous to the privileged confidentiality extended to doctors, lawyers, and clerics—by law in these cases) but not at the expense of societal devastation. Agencies should not be allowed to invade in any way without a warrant.

Copyright

Authors, publishers, and by devolution, database aggregators, hold actual or titular copyright to published material. The copyright owner has the right to profit from his or work. Stealing copyrighted material is unethical and illegal. Information does *not* want to be free. Information is produced at a cost. So, like Manning and Snowdon, who ostensibly aided society by committing treason (and theirs would have been unlawful acts even if the government were not involved), Aaron Swartz seemed to mean well, when he decided that all of those big, evil publishing companies should make everything available for nothing. There are valid arguments that can be made along this path, but illegally downloading the JSTOR database is not one of them. Swartz stole almost five million articles. At 26, he took the easy way out and committed suicide. This is a sad tale, but abrogating copyright and stealing, and in such an extreme fashion, is unacceptable, especially since his idea was probably to share the material with others at the expense of those named above and all of the libraries that subscribe to JSTOR. No sane person can seriously believe that one requires five million articles to do a research project. Ben Jackson, in a review of Swartz's *Boy Who Could Change the World,* makes many incisive points on both sides of this conundrum.

In the later part of the twentieth century, copyright was much out of date and so Congress authorized the Copyright Act of 1976. This extended copyright, which is good for authors and their heirs (unless a publisher has usurped the right), also made lots of people very nervous. Copy shops refused to help individuals, who had to do their own copying (so that they and not employees could go to jail), and even copy machines in libraries were outfitted with little signs warning people and students to avoid abrogation of the law, as they copied some pages of an article for their sixth grade projects. This is not theft; it merely makes matters more convenient and luckily the fair use doctrine allows for this, so individuals, shop owners, and librarians had little to fear. (Very few people copy *War and Peace* on a public copy machine.) Congress never rests, but rather continues to inundate us with laws, so in 1998, we were rewarded with the Digital Millennium Copyright Act (DMCA), which ratifies earlier treaties and protects against liability of service providers, among other things. Typical of the bizarre (and injurious) way in which legislators force irrelevancies onto laws, the DMCA, which essentially concerns data and the Internet, affects the hull design of certain vessels under its jurisdiction.

Copyright and other controlling legalities delimit global information justice. Two articles clarify the misapplication of copyright law and how the commodification of information harms Third World communities. First, Tomas Lipinski and Elizabeth Buchanan show how legal ownership rights impede informational flow through "the loss of the public domain" (47, 49). This stifles inquiry and so they demand balance for owners' and users' informational rights (57). Lamentably, this is unlikely to occur in the near future because of information commodification, capitalistic necessities, lobbying, and legislators sympathetic to corporate America (more than to individual creators) rather than to academic researchers and the public (which elected them).

Secondly, Johannes Britz and his coauthors insist that global capitalism harms Third World countries by denying informational justice. Commodification results in costs that even people in the West cannot accommodate; in poorer nations, housing, food, and medicine must take precedence over critical informational needs, and so information justice is denied. The solution is the authors' contention that in the developing world "access to essential information is more important than the right to own it" (67). This flies in the face of Western cultural and legal mandates as well as the balance that Lipinski and Buchanan advance. And the practical results of Britz's iconoclastic pronouncement are negligible. The only real alteration comes from the generosity of Western rights owners, an example of which is the reduction in rates or elimination of cost for important (medical) journals required in Third World libraries. This is helpful but it is dependent on charity rather than ethical or legal mandates. It is reminiscent of the exorbitant prices demanded for pharmaceuticals followed by the announcement that if one has a problem with payment, "AstraZeneca may be able to help." It would be more beneficial if it (and other drug companies) priced their products fairly while reducing their charitable inclinations.

Fair Use

Fair use gives one the right to appropriate certain amounts of copyrighted material. There are many caveats and controls, but the bottom line is that one may legally excerpt or reproduce shorter or longer texts and other media for various purposes. Here, as is often the case, the innocent are hounded while the abusers profit. Pirates in China or Thailand have no interest in the fair use doctrine; they just steal what they want. When a professor gives his or her students copies of a text or image that they would not purchase under any circumstance, and so there is no monetary loss to the author or artist, there can still be legal repercussions, which is what occurred in the 1991 Kinko's case (Basic Books, Inc. v. Kinko's Graphics Corp.) in which the shop reproduced excerpts from books; because of this, copy shops became chary of reproducing material.

It is apparently acceptable nevertheless for Google Books to include substantial amounts of text from individual books in its massive online collection. The Supreme Court refused to hear a challenge to this practice. Even placing a document on reserve in a university library became an issue, because the copyright holders were greedy and wanted to earn more money. Perhaps that is why some textbooks such as *Basic Inorganic Chemistry* cost $226.38, *Ethics in Business and Economics*, $550, *Biostatistical Genetics and Genetic Epidemiology*, $665, and *Comprehensive Toxicology* $7,085 (these examples came from a simple online search).

The essence of the fair use doctrine is quite simple; the articulated law, naturally, complicates matters, but with a minor effort, it is possible to understand what is necessary in order to achieve one's fair and legal end, especially in an educational setting. All of this is certainly ironic, since most Internet surfers do not bother with such niceties, but rather download or print whatever they encounter.

The Right to Be Forgotten

Because everything one does online is not only stored for future use, to market, sell, and surveil, but also made available to the general public via search engines (along with gossip and self-revelations on social media), even the non-thinking public, which does little to protect itself from privacy incursions, has rebelled. In the United States, things have not altered much, but in the European Union, the 1995 *Data Protection Directive* mandates that one has the right to be forgotten, one's data expunged, so that the verifiable fact that one once had a bar fight or purposely crashed her motorcycle into the Trevi Fountain, must be eliminated from search engine files. As noted above, failure to comply with a reasonable request can result in a 100 million Euro fine. This is an extravagant amount of money, but the EU legislators insist on compliance.

In the United States, we value privacy and people do not want their foolish past actions to haunt and damage them forever, but we also value freedom of speech. If everything that does not enhance us and our egos were to be expunged from all (publicly accessible) records, searchers would draw a bizarrely stilted picture of each individual. It is understandable that people should want to have the ability to get rid of negative, malicious, or false information, though they would probably balk if others did this, but it is equally comprehensible that we should probably not allow the wholesale extirpation of detrimental material, which would create a false picture and history.

We may have the desire to inhibit access, but we do not have a *right* to be forgotten. True human rights are extremely precise and limited. From a philosophical perspective, governments and organizations do not grant us rights. We hold certain inalienable rights (life, liberty, content-ment) merely by virtue of being human and in the same way that animals have certain rights merely by virtue of being sentient. That some of these rights in both cases are abrogated neither diminishes nor permanently extinguishes them. That these limited rights have not always been allo-cated fairly or justly does not change things; it merely indicates that in the past or in certain locations, human rights have been abrogated.*

These limited rights are also allocated and protected by government and enforced by law. Some people and documents may stretch rights to include many things that are warranted, desirable, and beneficial, but they are not inherent human rights, and the right to be forgotten is an extreme example. By including such a broad array of putative entitlements, the United Nations' *Universal Declaration of Human Rights* (which includes the right to trial, to move, to marry, to own things, to play—all positive

---

*For example, in China, parents sometimes threw their new-born daughters off a cliff because they desired male offspring in order to protect them in their old age. This custom was culturally accepted and, even if illegal, ignored by authorities. Nevertheless, it was an abrogation of the child's inalienable right to life; infanticide is a despicably evil action. It never was, is, or will be ethical to kill an innocent infant. Ethical relativism based in cultural customs and taboos is confirmed only by the habits themselves; it is a circular (and false) argument.

activities but not rights) vitiates those rights that are inherent by virtue of our humanity, and thus we do have the *right* not to be enslaved or tortured or have our thoughts and their expression stifled.

Even some of the "rights" enumerated in the Constitution's first ten amendments (the "Bill of Rights") are not really rights at all, for example, the eighth's, which adjures that "Excessive bail shall not be required, nor excessive fines imposed, nor cruel and unusual punishments inflicted." These are laudable sentiments, but hardly rights and they are abrogated with great frequency. A true right such as life or liberty can only in the most extreme situations be ignored or repudiated. When a barbarian commits a heinous crime, he or she loses the right to be part of society and so is penalized through imprisonment or execution, and as civilization has progressed, capital punishment (the abrogation of the right to life) has slowly been eliminated in many countries. Eventually, capital punishment will no longer be implemented, though this may take a century or two; human beings learn very slowly.

Rights inhere in us in the same way that physicality or physiology does. During human history they have merely been usurped by the powerful or greedy. (It might be noted that in addition to rights, we also have human obligations or duties.) The *right* to be forgotten is a myth; though we should have the ability to rid the record of false or harmful material, we do not have the right to create a false image, one that lacks the integrity of both truth and completeness. The EU obviously disagrees. Ironically, scholars have discovered that expunged information is sometimes recoverable: Researchers culled out 283 deleted articles from which 103 yielded 80 expunged names (Scott, "Researchers"). This thus turns out to be a rather ineffective process. Meg Leta Jones delineates the legal aspects of EU forgetting across various countries' different applications of its *Directive*. It is a messy business, because there are times when two competing social or ethical or legal necessities (privacy vs expression, in this case) create a dilemma, one that is difficult or impossible to resolve.

Detrimental and thus expungeable material exists in countless areas including newspaper morgues, archives, and government records but the issue is most salient in cyberspace. And here is a bifurcate problem: All of the tens of millions of personal webpages created through GeoCities were expunged so the data were lost, but not really, because they are still available in the Internet Archive, but the original owners of the pages did not know that their material would be available forever (Milligan), even if locked away in a location that most people do not visit. Here, apparently, forgetting is impossible.

Jones reminds us that computers are but the tip of the pyramid that contains "phones, cars, credit cards, televisions, household appliances, ... watches, and eyewear" among other sources of online data that might come to haunt one (8). Jones is sympathetic to those who wish to expunge and forget and so she reframes matters in terms of "digital redemption," "information stewardship," and forgiving (21, 80). The terminology is palliating; the results are the same, and here they are: In the first month that Google allowed forgetting in the EU, it received "70,000 requests to remove 250,000 links." It complied and a coincidental (roughly) 70,000 links were deleted (Jones 46).

In the United States, we are not as sanguine nor amenable to free speech incursions, but legal means do exist: "intellectual property restrictions; contractual obligations; defamation; and the privacy torts." Extralegal possibilities include code, social norms, and the market. Companies such as Reputation.com can remove negative material but this requires a payment (Jones 57, 73, 74). A balanced perspective on and implementation of forgetting procedures to protect privacy (vs. freedom of speech) may be necessary but very difficult to imagine. Garton Ash puts it this way: "... the notion of a generalised 'right to be forgotten' is indefensible in a society that believes in freedom of expression" (309). (See the fall 2018 issue of the *Journal of Information Ethics,* which is devoted to the topic.)

Secrets

The law likes to surprise. It takes years to study and many additional months to prepare for a bar examination to be legally entitled to act as a lawyer and more experience to become a judge. Nevertheless, the often quoted legal mandate "Ignorance of the law is no excuse" still holds some sway for the layperson. The law is complex and no one can know it in its entirety. Recently, the government has made matters more complicated by purposely concealing the law, an excellent example of a clash between ethical activity and unethical legality. Elizabeth Goitein observes that

FISA, intelligence agencies, and the President produce regulations that are not shared with the public, the result of which was torture and warrantless wiretapping. She calls for change and insists "that a regime of secret law has no place in a democracy." This is an informational failure.

The law takes a strong interest in the informational aspects of most matters that affect citizens, including privacy, security, finances, education, health, and the ability to access government material, which is facilitated in the United States by the 1967 Freedom of Information Act (FOIA)—an incursion into governmental secrecy inconceivable and unprecedented just a few years ago (except that Sweden managed to implement a similar law in 1766). It is a good idea and other nations have followed precisely in its footsteps; for example, there is a Nigerian FOIA. In fact, almost 100 countries have such laws, although even in the United States, it is difficult to get agencies to cooperate at all or to prevent their extirpating through marker pen the very data that one seeks. One might guess that access to proscribed government information in Zimbabwe, despite its law, may be difficult to achieve.

Naturally, the government is not the only entity to protect secrets and that is because secrecy itself protects against harm. Government and corporate secrets are held to be sacrosanct and attempts to ferret them out can result in arrest and conviction, although when *WikiLeaks* is responsible, no one does anything about it. But individuals are fully at risk and there exist online sites that will help one discover everything available on anyone—for a price. The data here are publicly available, but require some a priori knowledge and a great deal of work. These sites (for example, Pipl.com, 123People.com) do the work for you by aggregating diversely situated data, but expect some remuneration for their trouble. Naturally, the real secrets probably remain hidden.

See especially New York University's "Information Law Institute ... an academic center for the study of law, policy, and social norms defining and affecting the flow of information in a digitally networked society." And the July 2012 issue of *IRIE* is devoted to the "Ethics of Secrecy."

14 Academia and Its Discontents

Academia (higher education) is not what it once was: an idyllic urban (City College of New York, Yale) or rural (Cornell, Ohio University) campus that offered a welcoming environment where students and faculty at least attempted to get along in order to foster the learning process. Some young people went to school to study a subject that would lead to a career, but others attended just to learn with no thought to the future. Attitudes naturally depended on the economy, the individual's financial situation, and the cost, which ranged from free (Hunter College in the 1930s to reasonable (Wagner College in the '60s) to extremely expensive (Bennington College in the '70s).

Years rolled by smoothly with some few insurrections (world wars, civil rights and free speech movements, and Kent State murders), but the atmosphere was one in which a diligent student could learn without fear of reprisal or degradation because he or she held radical or heretical beliefs and articulated them. College was a place in which one might debate diverse propositions and attend guest lectures by outspoken thinkers: iconoclasts, bigots, or fools. Students did not live in mortal fear of expulsion for claiming that intelligent design is or is not valid and tenured faculty were not threatened with dismissal because they offended someone. (Well, perhaps that was not such a good situation because colleagues sometimes mistreated their peers horrifically.) Nevertheless, things have changed so dramatically in a short period that José Cabranes, a judge and former counsel for Yale, describes the academic environment as "the new 'surveillance university,'" where academic freedom and tenure are under attack and civility police control faculty and students.

127

The Scope of Information Ethics

Colleges and universities exist in order to provide instruction, not facilitate sports programs, publish monographs, train welders, or support an army of administrators. These are all peripheral; there is nothing wrong with football or mechanical skills but one went to school to get a liberal education. Since English fiction and historical theorizing no longer lead to remunerative positions, they are disrespected, and those who manage to graduate often remain ignorant of classic knowledge because it was produced by dead white males. But whatever is taught and learned comprises information and only that which is true and valid should be promulgated. Ideologues should not alter curricula to conform to their popular beliefs. Intellectual bullying has no place in the life of the mind. Jonathan Zimmerman discusses this and other matters in *Campus Politics*, in which he describes the students at Seattle University who were traumatized by the Western classics. The administration agreed to investigate. "If we resist the urge to pronounce the protesters insane and the administrators craven...," observes Zimmerman, then one must ask whether schools do harbor prejudicial attitudes (Marks).

In the nonacademic world, one finds human resource officials and little more. Here, students require offices staffed by hundreds of administrative assistants who specialize in disabilities, racial problems, minorities, sexual preferences, and so on. Some of these students need help and so the services are warranted, but others are merely coddled. And students demand trigger warnings, safe spaces, and protection from every conceivable microaggressive offensive affront, including speakers whose ideas they do not like and so they disrupt presentations. Academic freedom is under assault and both offending students and faculty are disciplined.

Caring and consideration for fellow human beings, especially in an informational environment, is admirable and failing to accommodate the offended is unethical. But schools have gotten carried away and cater to the fringe. Political correctness is an abomination. What is truly wrong is that a thoughtless remark can result in expulsion, but a rape can go unpunished, at school or in the courts, while the victim is blamed. Rape, like murder and kidnapping, is one of the vilest crimes and should be punished accordingly. Instead, it is ubiquitous and taken for granted. As for triggers, a caring instructor will always warn students that something horrific is on the way. Decades ago, this author indicated to an honors class that the

---

first part of a book was egregiously unpleasant, and he suggested that the squeamish skip it. He once showed the two reel film *Titicut Follies* to a class. After the first reel ended, the class requested an eternal hiatus from this cinematic mistreatment of the criminally insane. He acquiesced.

Colleges and universities have become battlefields because not everyone accepts demagogic control. The University of Chicago informed its 2016 freshman class that it would not tolerate a caring environment: College must not coddle but rather educate at any price including a student's sanity or life. Berkeley disagreed. So too do some activist organizations and students who fight back against this tide. Any form of intellectual suppression or censorship, especially at an academic institution, is anathema but psychological abuse or death is worse. In 2016, Pen America published a 102 page, 462 footnoted indictment of things gone wrong, especially attacks on freedom of speech, at American colleges and universities. It discusses all of the current issues as well as disinvited speakers, punishments, Title IX, and sexual harassment. Three case studies, at Yale, UCLA, and Northwestern, round out this plea for sanity in what has become a demented, uncivil environment (Pen passim).

A complaint that is often voiced, sometimes by people who have little to do with academia, is that most professors are liberals who forward a liberal and progressive informational agenda, one that often calls for advocacy and direct action. Conservatives feel left out, even frightened, and often maintain a low profile. There is some truth to this but it is because liberals choose education while conservatives opt for the legal profession, politics, economics, and especially business, where they can follow their own agendas and earn lots of money by exploiting others.

Exploitation occurs in the academic world as well, particularly in the harsh environs of high profile laboratories at research universities where grantsmanship and a program to win a Nobel Prize for the director may be more important than the useful knowledge ostensibly being produced. What is stunning here is that at pure research facilities, such as Lawrence Livermore National Laboratory, high ranking physicists abandon lab work, leaving it to doctoral students and post-docs, and spend their time writing up results, traveling around the world giving papers, and of course writing grant proposals. I doubt that these serious researchers have time to worry about political machinations and the reasons why they feel out of joint with their liberal or conservative colleagues. And, naturally, academic campuses do have their share of conservative instructors and young Republicans who set up tables in student unions and hope to seduce 17 year old freshmen into eventually voting for Nixon or Reagan or Trump.

One should never forget that conservative students at outstanding institutions (Dartmouth as a random example) sometimes have very unpleasant (racist, homophobic) things to say about others. In any case, it is unethical and should be illegal for anyone to discriminate against peers, subordinates, or overseers. Academic and intellectual freedom insist upon tolerance for offending ideas. This does not mean one must tolerate mendacity, harmful activities, or stupidity.

In late 2016, *The Chronicle of Higher Education* published a section devoted to "The Problem with Higher Education Is _____." A series of questions were posed to 48 people associated with academia, including Mark Bauerlein, Cathy Davidson, Amy Gutmann, and Judith Shapiro. Their answers varied in length from a sentence or two to a brief paragraph. There exist many problems: Credential inflation, cost, contingent workers, the business model, free speech, and political correctness exemplify this (passim).

One of the most controversial developments in academia (and business) is sexual harassment. It has become so ubiquitous that people ignore history and drastically confuse matters, for which they can perhaps be forgiven, since confirmed harassers, abusers, and even rapists get away with their transgressions and the victim is blamed and suffers. But two points should be considered. Campus romantic relationships are not necessarily abusive and in the not so distant past, these relationships among faculty, staff, and students were taken for granted. Things are different today, and rules with very severe penalties attempt to control these types of interactions. And of course it is not just faculty-student liaisons that bear rotten fruit; faculty members may also end up disliking, accusing, and suing each other.

Information plays a critical role here, because it reveals what occurred, how it is addressed, and who is believed. Often there is no available probative evidence, and the entire business may end up in court, based on personal accusations and counter-claims and gossip. It is a situation where there can be no winners, although many people are seriously damaged:

14. Academia and Its Discontents

Faculty are banned from teaching or the campus, forced to resign, or fired; they may sicken or die. Sometimes, all of this may derive from a vengeful partner who has dissimulated. Brian Leiter rhetorically wonders whether those found guilty should be permanently banned from teaching. He thinks not: As he notes, other professionals can start again. But things are more complicated. Hugging a secretary is not harassment but neither is rape; it is much worse. These terms are tossed around so frequently that they lose their meaning, and all one must do is present an accusation and the accused is deemed guilty.

Most of these negative interactions occur between students; often a male is accused of rape with an unconscious female who has consumed an overabundance of alcohol or drugs. It is thought that only a small percentage of these occurrences are reported and when they are, very little is done. A 2016 court sentence was so lenient that it created a national uproar. Rape, a crime that historically was considered by some to be worse than death and that should result in life imprisonment, is treated mildly or with contempt by the patriarchy that passes the laws.* In other countries, matters are even worse, and it is the victim who is guilty and punished. It is unethical and illegal to harass, abuse, or rape but it is also unethical and illegal to lie, to seek revenge through accusation when nothing untoward occurred. If possession or consumption of alcohol and drugs at academic institutions were grounds for immediate dismissal, even of consenting adults, then severe sexual abuse would be considerably reduced. Is such a bizarre measure possible?† Is it possible that tuition would rise from almost nothing or just a few thousand dollars to as much as $70,000 a year in just half a century? It has!

Things have also changed in institutional structure. Now instead of having one administrator for every 50 or 100 faculty members, there seem to be 10 administrators for each instructor. This explosion of administrative

---

*In Minnesota, pedophiles who seriously harm children either do not go to prison at all ("...65 percent of felony child rapists in Minnesota never spend a day in prison...") or get a 90 day to two year sentence (Du). Minnesota is a liberal state that cares about its citizens, but in this case, the mitigating legislation is extremely misguided.

†Shortly after writing this, *The New York Times* reported that the obscenely out of control consumption of alcohol on campuses is being curbed by new rules at "dozens of universities": games, kegs, and hard liquor are now sometimes prohibited. It is about time (*The New York Times* 14 Y).

duties and employees is one of the worst developments in American education, wasteful and burdensome, especially since an assistant professor might earn $75,000 a year whereas her dean makes 150,000. I am not certain that deans are truly necessary. Then there is the tenure/adjunct problem, which eventually will destroy American higher education and its well-founded reputation as the world's finest. It is harmful and unethical to distort, diminish, or stifle the flow of informational instruction by eliminating tenure track positions (and tenure) and hiring adjuncts who do not fully participate in the life of the department and institution, and who are underpaid and therefore feel unappreciated. They are, ironically, in the same position as unrepresented, non-unionized graduate assistants.

This litany of miseries is enough to deter even the most sympathetic person from defending the current state of academic affairs. Sadly, the worst is in the offing: The most nauseatingly repugnant aspect of American secondary and higher education today, the vilest breach of academic integrity and the ethical application of information, is the often unacknowledged and subsequently disbelieved extent of dishonest activity on the part of students including those engaged in writing dissertations. Students have cheated, cribbed, and plagiarized since the advent of formal education. This author was stunned, almost 60 years ago, as a college student, attending a class in a foreign "high school"; there, graduation would lead directly to the country's elite universities. These young adults had no ethical qualms and cheated on tests.

But things are much worse now: A high percentage of papers are produced not by the submitting student but by ghost writers who work for paper mills. If students required a philosophical basis for their transgressions they could cite the ghosts, sometimes not credited at all, responsible for celebrity memoirs, or their cousins, who are never credited on clinical trial reports and papers, which may appear in the best medical journals. But it is highly doubtful that these countless, unprincipled, deceitful students give any thought at all to their actions when ordering yet another English or history paper from a paper mill, for which they must pay substantial sums of money.

A number of former academic forgers have written books on the subject. Jeffrey Alfred Ruth informs us that as many as four million ghost-written papers are turned in each year. Ruth alone authored more than

300 of these pieces during a short period of time (9). The horrible part of all of this is that students are, of course, harming themselves; even though what they are doing is not illegal, it is *the* major breach of academic ethics and often grounds for failure or expulsion. No one really cares. More than 30 years ago, at a major research university, a friend accused her student of plagiary and it was the instructor who was harassed; it was so onerous to follow through on this, I seem to recall, that she dropped the charges.

Today, with the possibility of earning a degree partially or fully online, the opportunities for dishonesty are increased by many factors. There do exist ways to combat dishonesty and they include honor codes and pledges (but these do not work, even at the military academies), the elimination of papers, in-class composing and testing, and threats of extremely severe repercussions if caught. If this business reached a crisis in 2018, it was already problematic in the 1960s, when this author failed a student for blatant physical theft and plagiarism, which she would not acknowledge, and 30 years later when he stopped requiring papers except from advanced graduate students—not that they are incapable of turning in 40 or 50 page fraudulent theses. (See Clemson's International Center for Academic Integrity, which has hundreds of member institutions around the world. http://www.academicintegrity.org/icai/home.php).

---

15 Business

There exists a relatively small group of extremists, neither militants, private militiamen, survivalists, nor anarchists, who despise government, who hold that government is basically evil and other than some basic activities such as military protection, no matter what it does is superfluous. Everything should be privatized: education, transportation, postal delivery, entitlements such as Medicare and especially social security (an insurance policy rather than a Ponzi scheme), which happens to support one fifth of the population and keeps low income people off the welfare rolls (but which this group thinks should be expunged). These are the libertarian minded, the Randian Objectivists, the entrepreneurs, the little and big business people who have been seduced by free market ideologies, the type of nonsense promulgated by Milton Friedman who informs us that the **only** loyalty a business or business person has is to stockholders.

These people denigrate the government and its laws and regulations that attempt to protect citizens, while insisting that it is capitalist business and free markets that are good, caring, and helpful despite their greed, gouging, exploitive nature, and mechanical responses to human crises. But both of these positions are bizarrely extreme, misleading, and false. Government and business both serve and without the former a large country such as the United States would devolve into anarchy; the diminution of business would have an equally humbling effect on production and innovation. Venezuela is a good example of what can go wrong when a political and economic ideology runs amok; Syria offers the same lesson from a dictatorial perspective.

Business does almost nothing for government but government supports business with financial aid and helps to rein in and control the many bad incentives that business by its very nature ensures. That government gets carried away by insisting on licensing hair braiders or insinuating foolish OSHA regulations where they are unnecessary or harmful in no way diminishes the unequivocal need for strict regulation in virtually every area, from airline transportation to the production of meat and other foodstuffs. Informational breaches contaminate every major type of business, including agricultural machinery manufacturers, the pharmaceutical industry, insurance, health care, retail, and especially commercialized online marketing and sales. Unethical informational overload can occur in every aspect of capitalist business processes—research, discovery, patenting, trolling, manufacturing, marketing, seducing, selling, and exploiting everyone along the creation, wholesaling, distribution, and disseminating chain. Businesses exist to earn a profit; even nonprofit organizations profit and pass the money on to their executives: Elizabeth Dole earned $200,000 as president of the American Red Cross and other executives at similar nonprofits earn a great deal more. Earnings come to dominate every decision and the stock price of publicly owned companies surges and diminishes based on profit predictions and margins. It is an unsavory mess.

Many areas and instances bear discussion. The single worst manifestation of falsification, long before fake news emerged from the political swamp, is the tobacco industry's lies concerning the harm that one suffers from the use of tobacco products. The informational barrage that the major companies spewed out comprised a purposeful and concerted effort to convince smokers through blatant deception. Tobacco executives at the major companies knew full well that countless harms accrue from smoking and chewing tobacco, but cared even less than the Ford Motor Company administrators who preferred to pay large sums of money to those people harmed or killed in Pinto explosions rather then redesign the faulty automobile. (The Chevrolet Corvair also had major safety problems; see Ralph Nader's *Unsafe at Any Speed*.) Note that tobacco is said to have killed 100 million people in the twentieth century. To make matters much worse, The Heartland Institute, a horrible think tank that functions as a mouthpiece for the self-serving corporations (e.g., Philip Morris, Koch, ExxonMobil) that fund it, created attractive brochures assuring its readers that tobacco is harmless; this is the same group that insists that global warming is a myth. What the naive person in the street, the consumer, must come to understand is that businesses wish to sell products and if this entails the dissemination of blatantly false claims, then that is a small price to pay for all of the money that rolls in from packs of cigarettes (which not so long ago cost 25 cents but which now sell for ten dollars) and fossil fuels.

Ideologically motivated free market entrepreneurs start with a farrago of basic a priori axioms (government is bad, business is good) and then must contort their beliefs to conform to the axioms. So, Rachel Carson's *Silent Spring* cannot be correct because it harms corporations; global warming is a myth because compassionate companies would never pollute and cause the atmosphere to degenerate; toxins in herbicides and pesticides are harmless; and so on. This type of irrational reasoning is responsible for much of the misery in the world and the wealth garnered by the rich (Jeff Bezos, the Walton family) at the expense of the exploited worker (see Barbara Ehrenreich's *Nickel and Dimed* and Head's *Mindless*).

In order for consumers to react positively to corporate offerings, they must place their trust in the integrity of the business. Lamentably, many corporations no longer value integrity and so it is very difficult to trust what they proffer. Despite this, the naive learn that Humira and other frequently advertised medicinals are life saving and therefore ask their physicians for a prescription. They ingest the drug and die. This is not how medical care should function. If they survive, their purchasing information and other little and big data derived from cookies and other sources are sold to other firms. Then the innocent purchaser or Internet surfer is bombarded with targeted solicitations to buy ever more garbage.

A small group of businesses prey on the unwary, maligned, sickened, or downtrodden and take advantage of the naive. They include payday lenders, which charge usurious rates of interest and harm the borrowers who can never catch up with their payments; debt settlement companies, which seduce through misleading claims and may charge despite the fact that they accomplish nothing; law firms that specialize in certified class action law suits and take a hefty percentage of the award that the disabled person needs to survive (when he or she should be able to collect with no legal representation) and advertise obnoxiously on television for victims of mesothelioma, automobile injuries, or social security denial (and to think it was once considered unethical for the legal profession to advertise!).

Production

The production of manufactured goods has always been fraught with misery for those who worked in plants or on assembly lines. Henry Ford paid his employees well, but others did not until unions came along to help the afflicted. Corporate administrations have the habit of not sharing information, failing to indicate forthcoming alterations until one day a pink slip appears in one's pay envelope, the company simply closes, or in the worst case, an employee is told to leave immediately and is locked out. There are many considerations that must obtain when making decisions, but it is ethically reprehensible to keep loyal workers in the dark until the moment when the guillotine falls. This is especially salient now when robotics is altering the workforce. A robotic welding arm that replaces a worker is very different from valued workers who are assured that artificial intelligence will not really eliminate jobs because it will create new ones. But I think that this is overly optimistic. As the population increases, the number of available positions will diminish. Precise data and information should be shared by employers as they automate (or shift their production out of the country).

Marketing

Corporate marketers are charged with the task of getting a product into the hands of paying consumers. The means with which this is accomplished varies along an ethical scale and includes fair and honest informational dissemination, but also deceptions, scams, and sexual seduction as in the automobile ads of the distant past, which have made a comeback, in which scantily clad females lean on or wash various brands of cars. It is hard to believe that sophisticated Americans fall for such nonsense but they do: Buy a Mustang or BMW and this lovely woman might wash it for you.

Advertising

The primary way in which corporate marketers reach potential consumers through their marketing departments is by advertising in all media including newspapers and magazines, radio, television, billboards (where legal; in some locations, such as Vermont, they are not), and especially now, the Internet, which insinuates extremely annoying ads whenever one attempts to do some legitimate work. At times, even software fails to filter out this rubbish. Many people do wish to purchase things and do fall for the advertisements (and buy another iPhone every year or two), but there are also those who neither require nor desire a new car, a fancy gown, or shampoo. Nevertheless, they must suffer through the bombardment, if they wish to view a video, read a scholarly paper, or confirm a fact digitally. Pop-ups, spam, and fake enticements take a large toll on society.

Whereas in the past, newspaper and magazine ads might have taken up a small percentage of pages, they now overwhelm with immediacy; some legitimate publications may consist almost exclusively of solicitations to buy, sell, or proffer, and advertorials can confuse even the sophisticated. At one time, television programs were interrupted once or twice for a brief moment or two to sell some product. Today, it is not impossible to sit through as many eleven consecutive pleas for the interrupted viewer to purchase everything from insurance, foodstuffs, soap, pharmaceuticals, and cosmetics to appliances and automobiles. Some of the hawkers are so offputting that a sensitive person is forced to turn them off. All of this comprises a subset of irritating informational overload, but this is hardly the entire story.

Much that is touted in ads and commercials is distorted, propagandized, or false. A truly egregious example, noted above, is the tobacco industry's claim that smoking does not cause illness. This could be ascribed to a disingenuous attitude, if one were sympathetic and inclined to be generous or forgiving, but it has been unequivocally shown that tobacco consumption is a direct cause of many physical ailments including cancer. Impossibly, there has been an upsurge of interest in smoking as marijuana has become legalized, more acceptable, and popular in many areas. Smoking this product cannot be good for the lungs which originally evolved to process oxygen. Many of the claims made generally for almost any product may be so exaggerated as to be untrue. Every watch, insurance company, or popular film cannot be the very best in the history of humankind.

Advertising employs many behavioral tricks and gimmicks to convince readers and viewers to do something or purchase a product that they neither need nor want. The uncontrollably susceptible watch home purchasing networks and buy until their houses are flooded with "goods." If all of this were not bad enough, we now have "stealth advertising," which Mara Einstein discusses in a recent study: We are deceived and tricked on a degraded World Wide Web through "hidden commercial propaganda" to purchase (Wu); here the key word is tricked.

Drug companies are notorious for unethical information dissemination. They claim that the cost of research is excessive, though much of it takes place at academic institutions, and they therefore must charge exorbitant amounts of money for basic drugs such as insulin or epinephrine, which is found in an EpiPen, a life-saving device for those who can succumb to an allergic reaction to seafood or an insect sting. Although drug firms now conclude their television pleas for purchase with a litany of counter-indications, perhaps because they have been sued or because the government mandates it, these are not really that important and the indication is that the use of the medicine would be quite beneficial. A high percentage of potential medicinal drug users ignore warnings for heart attack, stroke, seizures, or even death.

And it is good to keep in mind the ways in which pharmaceutical research results are disseminated: A company employee summarizes what has been discovered and this is passed on to a professional medical writer, who, for an extraordinary fee, writes up the work in a formal paper, which is then published in *JAMA* or *The Lancet*. These ghost-written papers are "authored" by doctors, some of whom have almost nothing to do with the research or the report. This then becomes part of the historical record and it helps to sell drugs and enrich a limited group of people. Sometimes, the data and their implications are misleading or false.

The blatantly deceptive information that pharmaceutical companies such as Pfizer, GlaxoSmithKline, Schering, Merck, and Proctor and Gamble purposely tender in prescription drug ads has resulted in government censure. At least this was the case from 1998 through 2002, during which time one author (Pear) noted that the FDA presented 88 letters of complaint.

Ironically, a group of Russian thieves figured out how to elicit millions of dollars a day from advertisers: It is a very complicated scheme but it boils down to tricking large companies into paying for video ads that are then placed on 250,00 fake sites; bots click constantly so that it appears as if everyone in the universe is reading this junk whereas in reality, few if any humans set eyes on these calls for purchasing. Fox News, CBS Sports, *The New York Times, The Wall Street Journal*, Facebook, and Yahoo were among the many organizations deceived. In 2016, Internet advertising fraud wasted more than seven billion dollars (Goel passim). The commercialized Internet, which originally was to be a communication network free of capitalistic seductions, has become a haven for theft and harm.

Banking and Investment

It is no secret that banking, even at its best, can be a sordid business. High interest rates and foreclosures in the past have harmed individuals and families, farmers and businessmen, while bankers have enriched themselves. More recently, financial institution bankruptcies could have destroyed the economy except that they were rescued by government infusions. Wells Fargo did highly unethical and illegal things but continues to prosper; Bernard Madoff stole billions of dollars. Bankers and investment advisors proffer misleading and false information and balk when a potential law demands that the latter group place their clients' interests before their own. Credit reports control the destinies of the less fortunate as well as the striving middle class which is forced to borrow, perhaps undertake a reverse mortgage, trade equity for fast cash, and sometimes leave their heirs with debt. The wealthy have no need for credit or reports. They can pay cash (or bitcoin; see below). Here is the horror: When an inadvertent error seeps in, it is very difficult to correct it. The three credit bureaus do not care very much for the people who generate all of their income and they certainly do not protect the private data that they acquire, against many people's desires.

In a bizarre development, the marketing of cybercurrencies such as Bitcoin is a superb example of an unethical informational deluge (perhaps a scam) that ultimately will cause a great deal of financial harm. The impossibly ongoing inflating price of these computer-generated, digital assets has been compared with the tulip bulb mania of the seventeenth century. This is a foolish parallel: A tulip bulb is a physical object that one can buy, sell, hold, plant, and watch bloom. It has some intrinsic value. Cybercurrencies exist only on computer servers located in distant cooled-down locations and in the minds of those who believe in them.

Insurance

The insurance business might under the right circumstances be considered a scam. People pay billions of dollars in premiums to insure their dwellings, possessions, jewelry, art works, automobiles, liability, health, lives, yachts, crops, goods in transit, and many other things. Lloyds of London will insure anything. The premiums can be extremely high. Then along comes a destructive flood or earthquake or similar act of god or a bit of mold or asbestos or termites and so one finally gets around to scrutinizing the ten separate policies gathering dust in the vault only to discover that these things are excluded from coverage. Even governmental Medicare can make a fuss about certain procedures, although generally it does a fair job of protecting our aging population from the onslaughts of exorbitant medical costs. Consider that a simple MRI scan no longer costs one thousand dollars but can reach six times that amount. To be fair, the informational aspects here are laid out in the policy, but very few people read these documents carefully; additionally, companies do pay when warranted. Still, the informational aspects of insuring could be improved especially by simplifying policies.

Social Media

Facebook and its siblings provide services that for many people now appear to be indispensable. But these corporations are in business to earn large sums of money for their owners, and they do. That is why Facebook's young CEO is now the world's fifth wealthiest human being. Meanwhile, these online social interactions, which even young children take for granted, are fraught with unethical communications—information that is ugly and bullying, sexual and racist, threatening and extremely harmful.

Food

Correct and complete information concerning the food that both humans and animals consume has often in the past been purposely proscribed. The less we know about ingredients and nutritional value, the better off are the purveyors. Things changed when the government stepped in with legal demands and sanctions. Offal and toxins are no longer tolerated and manufacturers must list all ingredients in descending order of content as well as nutritional value percentages—including carbohydrates, fats, cholesterol, and vitamins. In this way, a purchaser can make a thoughtful decision. More recently even restaurants have been adjured to include some basic nutritional data on their menus or boards. Since a very high percentage of consumers eat at fast food emporia and purchase junk to consume at home, it might appear that only a limited number of people care about and consult the data on packaged food. But this may be untrue. One often observes people reading labels in stores, something that never happened a half century ago. Sinclair's *Jungle may* no longer exist, but there is still room for improvement. And animals are still overloaded with superfluous antibiotics and hormonal chemicals. In order to avoid these things in one's diet, it is necessary to pay strict attention to what one eats.

Concluding Remarks

Business is beneficial, although it is good to keep in mind the British aristocracy's former attitude to earning money commercially: it is gauche. These folks lived on inherited wealth and the services of their peasants who worked on the estate and shared their profits with the duke or count or baron. When the modern dukes of industry earn large sums of money they do everything in their power to discover ways (ethical, legal, otherwise) to protect it from the tax collector. They move to Ireland, incorporate in foreign duchies, and hide assets in Switzerland or Caribbean tax havens that specialize in such unethical and illegal practices. I know a person whose million dollars thus saved was confiscated by the United States; he did not seem overly concerned. More offensive is the example of Apple, which secreted $250 billion on the island of Jersey, a tax haven near France. The business community can be quite unsavory, that is, morally disreputable. Information always plays a seminal role—for good or evil.

16   Medicine

Medical ethics attempts to control physicians' practices. "First, do no harm!" is an excellent imperative but fails miserably when an insoluble dilemma presents itself, something that occurs all too frequently when health is concerned. If medication and surgery are the two most impressive and useful adjuncts to doctoring, information dispensing is an affirming third. Indeed, if patients paid attention to the available information provided in a host of venues, the person requiring serious treatment would probably not have had to see a doctor at all. Not every ailment is preventable by making good choices, but a plague of miseries could be avoided if human beings (including young children, adolescents, adults, and the elderly) acted in a rational manner and stopped smoking, eating harmful foods and to excess, consuming too much alcohol and recreational drugs, avoiding exercise, and participating in extremely stressful situations.

But people do not act rationally and with their own best interests in mind, and, additionally, many diseases and ailments are uncontrollable since they derive from genetic proclivity, visits to locales where dengue fever or ebola are raging, or accidents which break bones or tear ligaments.

But even here, where a visit to the doctor is mandated and information flows forth on what one should do, there is a failure—because like a dog that pulls out its stitches, people do what they want. They fail to rest after knee surgery or refuse to follow through on the entire course of antibiotics or conversely, they fall for the barrage of television commercials and ingest pill after pill in order to lose weight, increase their brain power, and "cure" a host of annoying and distressing problems, none of which warrant the powerful and dangerous medications available.

Education

For doctors, informational problems begin in college pre-med programs where the academic demands are overwhelming, the competition so intense that students cheat and rivals subvert their peers' work and experiments. The key to success is ever more information and knowledge—of biology, chemistry, anatomy, physiology, and clinical work for volunteers and EMTs; even high school students can participate in a candy striper program or Medquest, which allows them to shadow medical professionals. The goal is to acquire as much knowledge as possible in order to earn a very high GPA and to perform well on the MCAT.

Those who survive and enter medical school face four years of rigorous study and clinical work. A single, simple failure to learn a basic fact or procedure can cost a patient a leg or a life, so the pressure is always on, creating stress and sleepless nights, while more and more data and information are forced into the student's overburdened memory. Most people who enter medical school graduate: a little more than 80 percent in four years but 96 percent for those who drag it out for ten. Next comes a hospital internship followed by residency. Depending on the course of study, these can add three to seven years to the program. Information is power and the most successful new doctors are the ones who know the most and work the hardest. But the power fades because these doctors are forced to work 80 to 100 or more hours per week. The only thing they end up caring about is not information or ministering to the sick or hurt, but rather a decent meal and especially sleep.

In the past, hospital administrators were former clinicians; this has changed and now hospitals are controlled by hordes of superfluous business people (analogous to deans in the academy). Nevertheless, this barbaric system is kept in place by the very doctors who have suffered through it; they could rebel once they are settled into their profession and are invited back to profess at teaching hospitals. Apparently, they have more important things to do than protect the well-being of the young men and women who have dedicated their lives to the healing professions or their patients who must put up with diagnosis and surgery performed by people literally falling asleep on their feet. This is an ethical lapse of egregious proportions. And if it is not bad enough, anyone different is going to be mistreated by peers and especially conservative, misogynistic senior physicians. Elizabeth Morgan makes this clear in *The Making of a Woman Surgeon*, published in 1980, but things may hardly be much better today.

Misinformation

The major information ethics lapse in medicine is tendered and accepted misinformation—from deceptive pharmaceutical companies, practitioners with agendas, crackpots who advocate useless and sometimes harmful practices, and careless physicians who not only fail to help but who introduce infection or sponges into the body (iatrogenic problems fail doubly since they negate the Hippocratic Oath philosophically and cause real harm). There has always been a great deal of hokum in medicine. When people are ill or in pain, they are willing to try anything, from snake oil remedies long ago to a host of idiocies today. Practitioners introduced evidence-based medicine (EBM), a concept that one might presume would appeal to any rational person. A drug or procedure is shown to have a positive effect in a statistically significant number of cases (not just in one's neighbors' chickens) and so it makes sense to implement it, guided by a physician. But sometimes even the rationally knowledgeable balk and demean EBM and seem to prefer something euphemistically termed alternative or complementary or fringe medicine.

There is no such thing as alternative medicine. If something works, it becomes part of the medical armamentarium; if it does not have any positive effect, it is hokum. None of this matters to the true believer (in alternative facts?). Things shown to have little or no positive effect such as apricot pits, homeopathy, Christian Science (which advocates prayer over medical intervention), as well as traditional healing rituals of indigenous peoples and their shamans and botanical remedies are usually of little true medical value or act as a placebo, which sometimes allows the mind to effect a cure.

Every once in a while, it appears as if something derided by the American Medical Association (AMA) seems to work. Hollywood is quite partial to such miracles and so it turns out movies such as *Lorenzo's Oil*, *Extraordinary Measures*, and *First Do No Harm*. Positive results or those that appear to work may give false hope to others suffering from similar maladies. It is unfair and unjust to diminish hope for someone who is suffering, who wants to prolong a life, but it is equally horrendous to offer hope or scam or hoax the afflicted with fraudulent cures and quackery.

Those who accept and act upon misleading, false, or purposely fraudulent information forwarded by hoaxers, who prey upon the desperate who wish to help their children or parents or palliate their misery, may be self-serving quacks. But it is also possible that these people sincerely believe in their methods. That is why the government attempts to regulate medical interventions. It sometimes fails. It is difficult to acquire powerful medicinals, which may have an extremely harmful or deadly effect, without a prescription. But anyone can walk into a traditional "pharmacy" in New York's Chinatown and request a broad array of powders, which are then wrapped in small pieces of paper. Even those knowledgeable in their traditional use and application may find that they have little real effect or conversely these derivatives may harm or kill.

Confidentiality

The three traditional professions (medical, legal, clerical) offer legal protection for interactions. Privileged information may not be demanded even by a court and a professional who abrogates confidentiality may be criticized, penalized, and not trusted in the future. The apocryphal tale of the priest who learns of a bomb in the church's basement but refuses to break the sanctity of the confessional, and, as noted above, allows his parishioners to explode, offers extreme verification of how important confidences are to those whom we most trust with our destinies. Medical data and information can have a broadly negative physical and social effect on a person and so it is assumed that only those who truly have a need to know that one is genetically susceptible to Huntington's or Tay-Sachs disease will be granted this information, and this should not include insurance companies which can then deny coverage.

But this is not how the medical world works, despite the good intentions of practitioners. One day, I was sitting in an examination room whose walls were constructed of tissue paper. Much to my dismay, I could hear everything going on next door. I was so overcome with disgust that I wrote to the *New England Journal of Medicine* which published my lament. This type of inadvertent revelation is compounded by doctors discussing (gossiping about) patients, mistaken revelations to those who have no business knowing our secrets, and the recent addition of electronic medical recording, which brings with it a host of distasteful problems including wastefulness, lack of attentive interaction with patients, and the broad revelation of proscribed information especially to anyone with access to the computer system as well as pharmaceutical sales representatives, who can then target a patient for a specific medicine, and hackers, who breach systems, steal data, and demand ransoms. As with errors in credit reports, it may be difficult to make corrections, and when a legitimate but superseded ailment is till visible many years later, the patient may be unaware of the potential harm it can do with insurance companies, employers, and the justice system.

It is for these reasons that Congress decided that yet another cumbersome, and annoying statute should be implemented and so we are now burdened with HIPAA, a broad ranging law (occupying far too many pages) that professes, in part, to protect our privacy—by having us read a document and signing it! It is doubtful that it is truly effective. Laws are sometimes useful. Better are respectful and caring practitioners and technological protections. The best solution to online incursions is to store data on systems that are not accessible via the Internet. This is most disadvantageous and few organizations are willing to inconvenience themselves despite the potential harm to patients who place their trust in their integrity and care.

Information

And HIPAA is not helpful when physicians and mental health workers choose a search for patient information that the patient prefers to disallow. In the past, such a search would have been extremely difficult and often impossible to accomplish. Today, it is all easily available with a simple Internet search or if buried, through an online company that specializes in agglomerating individual data and selling it to anyone. It is highly unethical for medical practitioners to do this even if it is in the best interest of the patient. It is reminiscent of a point made in Robert Lindner's 1955 collection *The Fifty-Minute Hour*: Psychiatrists are not allowed to visit patients in their homes even though, at the time, doctors often made house calls. Lindner did and made a crucial discovery. And it is ethically questionable for a layperson to now do something that is ubiquitous: personal searching for medical information anywhere online. Material located on *Medline* or other medical databases may yield legitimate and useful material, but general searches on Google, for example, may turn up controversial information that a naive person will be unable to evaluate. Acting upon it may be harmful. And is it really necessary to repeat that medical professionals should not participate in any way as monitors of or advocates for torture, no matter how worthy the objective appears to be? Medical professionals' first duty is to the welfare of others, especially their patients. Here, the ethical application of information is of essential importance.

17   Architecture
and Engineering

Architecture

It is not difficult to design and build a house. I know, because I did both of these things basically by myself using hand not power tools. Naturally, correct information and its ethical application is critical here, because the success of the venture depends on precise and proper positioning, concrete, materials, physical construction, masonry, wiring, plumbing, and a host of minor details. Professional architects must take all of these things into consideration in order to avoid a debacle even with a normal private home. Potential disasters multiply dramatically when one designs a 75 story skyscraper. The American Institute of Architects' (AIA) *2017 Code of Ethics and Professional Conduct* delineates obligations to many constituencies, but the very first ethical standard is to informational competence: "Members should strive to improve their professional knowledge and skill" (AIA 1).

Here is a very simple example of how information can be used in an unethical way when positioning a building, and this has nothing to do with feng shui. California is notorious for mudslides. This, however, does not deter architects from cooperating in emplacing homes in dangerous locations, hundreds of them on a steep Oakland side hill. Some years ago, they rolled down the slope in a sea of mud, the same type of mud that destroyed homes and took almost 20 lives in early 2018. If the concrete used in the foundation is adulterated with sand or pebbles or the building is put together shabbily or the wiring is misconnected, the house may shift, fail to withstand a minor earthquake, or an electrical fire may consume it.

---

17. Architecture and Engineering

In 2017, London's Grenfell Tower fire killed 79 people who were trapped inside what appeared to be a fire-proof building, since it rose 24 stories and had no fire escapes. Building codes control small wooden apartment buildings (and even private houses require fire stop—that is, horizontal 2 × 4s between the studs inside the walls, which slows down flames from spreading upward); complex fire alarm systems and smoke detectors and sprinklers are often mandated. Grenfell was built out of ostensibly fire-proof materials (such as steel, concrete, aluminum, stone) that should have limited the spread of fire to the belongings of the inhabitants. But the architects and the contractors went astray (and criminal charges are possible) and used combustible material for insulation and cladding connectors and the result was a deadly debacle similar to what one sees in the 1974 Hollywood 138-story *Towering Inferno*.

Looking at images of the burning Grenfell Tower is a horrifying experience knowing that the building was gutted and 74 people died unnecessarily—the entire catastrophe due to a series of unethical informational decisions probably advanced to save money. When a literary critic acts unethically, no one suffers; when a doctor stumbles, a single individual may be harmed; but when an architect blunders negligently, very bad things can occur. In addition to the primary obligations owed to the public, the client, and the profession, architects, like the engineers who follow below, have a secondary commitment to society and ecological soundness.

Not all architectural and construction mishaps are quite so dramatic and painful: Roofs are ripped off houses in wind storms, balconies fall from skyscrapers onto sidewalks (and pedestrians), floods and tornadoes wreak havoc in locations that should not be inhabited—sometimes a great deal of havoc.

Engineering

The three traditional types of engineering (civil, mechanical, and electrical) have expanded and clones now include electronics and software and computer hardware engineers. Thus, engineering is an expansive term and covers extremely diverse tasks. In a certain sense, there is very little contiguity between a person who designs and constructs roads or ships and someone who creates aeronautical software or the infrastructure for a mobile phone system in a Third World country. And chemists and physicists are seconded by chemical and electronics engineers respectively, which results in very indefinite boundaries. But what all of these professions have in common is a commitment to the ethical application of information. As is often the case, though, things sometimes fail dramatically.

Excellent bridges have been designed for millennia and some Roman bridges and aqueducts are still in use. We have the knowledge of hundreds of years of diverse modern bridge building techniques, textbooks, and discussions, tables, and charts that lay out everything from the coefficient of expansion for different materials to the effect of wind sheer. But in 1940, something vey difficult to explain occurred: Just a few months after the Tacoma Narrows Bridge opened, it began to sway even more than it had and eventually it broke apart and crashed into the water below. New York's Brooklyn and Manhattan bridges are still standing after more than 100 years as are the more recent Golden Gate and George Washington structures. The inexplicable Tacoma disaster must be ascribed to an informational failure perhaps without precedent (see the amazing recording of this debacle at https://www.youtube.com/watch?v=XggxeuFDaDU). In early 2018, a 1500 foot cable-stayed bridge under construction in a Colombian mountain gorge collapsed; ten workers fell 900 feet to their deaths. The images are overpoweringly horrifying (Karasz).

Incredible as it may seem otherwise responsible engineers and construction workers have failed once again to take into account the easily available data and information when constructing a simple footbridge. Architects such as Frank Gehry and especially Santiago Calatrava design extremely complex buildings that are then constructed and do not fail in any way. Calatrava's Milwaukee Art Museum, with its movable roof and the many large stadiums that have roofs that open and close do not collapse.

This was not the case with the pedestrian bridge being constructed on the Florida International University campus in March of 2018. It collapsed before it was completed and several people were killed. The system used here, "accelerated bridge construction," in which the 174 foot bed was built on the side of the span and then set in place, has many advantages and it has been used successfully in the past (Mazzei et al.), but it would not be allowed in certain venues. Even prefabricated concrete beams may be disallowed despite the fact that on-site pouring increases the time that streets and roads are closed.*

There is now no valid excuse for structural collapse. Even destruction from earthquakes has been circumvented. The Florida International collapse was a horrible unnecessary tragedy, especially since the authorities had pertinent information that indicated a potential problem, but they concluded that the crack that was discovered "...did not compromise the structural integrity of the bridge" (Mazzei). This is a major ethical breach in engineering design and in the usage of substandard materials. There are more examples. *Engineering.com* reports on five of the very worst disasters: Chernobyl, Bhopal (toxic gas killed more than 13,000 people), the *Titanic*, the *Challenger*, and *Apollo 13*. Ethics matters.

Here is why: Engineering debacles, the result of faulty (unethical) decision-making and/or corruption, are obviously not merely occurrences of the distant past. On August 14, 2018 (which happened to be the present author's 77th birthday), the enormous Morandi bridge in Genoa Italy collapsed, killing 43 people. In 2017, an engineering professor informed the bridge's managing company that corrosion was in evidence; he made specific recommendations but no one followed up. The year before, another professor recommended "that the entire bridge be replaced (Glanz *passim*). Indeed, it was infamous for its repair history. If no data or information had been available then accusations of unethical activity could not be leveled, but here obviously this is not the case. (See https://www.you tube.com/watch?v=gefkuuNOCf4 for an explanation and https://www.youtube.com/watch?v=Y6suQ0FIoIQ for a simulation of the collapse.)

A salient problem, which might be called the software paradox, concerns the allocation of ethical responsibility for computer catastrophes. Most educated people have undoubtedly heard a line that is palliating but false: The computer erased the file, misdirected an email, computed incorrectly. It is easy to blame an inanimate object but anything that a device does can be traced back to a programmer. When a glitch or bug causes a problem (and a real problem such as a mistaken missile launching can

---

*Some years ago, the main street in Brattleboro, Vermont, was closed for many months because the state mandates that the entire bridge's concrete must be poured on site. This naturally results in a much more solidly anchored and therefore stronger structure.

have devastating effects), the fault may lie with the program, code, software, or hardware—all designed and created by human beings who ultimately must bear responsibility.

Two specialties are especially prone to dangerous purposeful failures that may lead to horror and annihilation. Chemical engineers create toxins and explosives that harm foliage (agent orange) and sentient life including innocent human beings (land mines, sarin). Chemical agents were dispersed in the First World War and again in various recent venues such as Syria. Nuclear engineers design and maintain power plants but also bombs and triggers. We should take care.

Ethics has always held an honored place in both medicine and law, and ethical sensitization is part of the pedagogical process, since in both professions an error can be fatal. Patients and clients depend on the good offices of both doctors and lawyers. Education for architects and engineers places an inordinate emphasis on technical matters and rightly so. But it is probable that even today, after some innovative changes, ethical sensitization within architectural programs is not of the highest importance. The same may be said for engineering despite mandatory requirements. When engineers can purposely subvert a system in order to present patently false data, as occurred in the Volkswagen scandal, it is obvious that ethical training in engineering is lacking. Volkswagen is strikingly culpable because the alteration of pollution data allowed 11 million cars to cause general societal harm over an extended period. If the German and American governments had any real power, they should have dismantled the company. Instead, a paltry $2.8 billion fine was levied and VW continues to sell cars.

Similar to many professions' codes, The National Society of Professional Engineers *Code of Ethics for Engineers* (https://www.nspe.org/resources/ethics/code-ethics) attempts to control the ways in which engineers operate. It can only be as effective as those who adhere to its strictures, which include encouragements to honor truthfulness. (See *Science and Engineering Ethics,* an exemplary publication that covers ethics in engineering to some extent.)

18   Expert Systems, Robotics, War

Some of this study's concerns have spread onto areas in which in the recent past this would have been unthinkable. Technology has progressed to a point at which thinkers ascribe consciousness, thought, and agency to inanimate objects, while concomitantly eliminating these defining characteristics from sentient creatures. This simply indicates that people get carried away with their foolish and misguided beliefs. It is necessary only to manifest simple common sense in order to realize (if realization is really required) that there exists an unbridgeable distinction between biological life and the simulated existence of inanimate objects, no matter how sophisticated they appear to be. Humans cannot impart complex life to entities in which it does not naturally inhere. The algorithmic, mechanical reactions of expert systems can act as a paradigmatic exemplar for the other entities discussed in this chapter.

Expert Systems

Although (information) technology is only one of the many areas in which ethics is operative, it is of course extremely important. It is all too easy to abuse the recently arrived devices, denuded of any precisely germane social or ethical strictures, which, when imposed upon us, often do little good. Even five year old kindergarteners soon learn that they can do really cool things with the technology afforded to them. Who does not want to play violent video games and kill enemies and monsters? Unless potent reasons are offered, these children grow up unconvinced that acting correctly is its own reward. Sometimes legal and judicial oversight serve when ethical threats turn out to be inadequate. Professionals who use sophisticated devices may resemble their five year old selves. Good things can be accomplished with imaging systems, tele-surgery, computerized stock trading, and expert systems, but the potential for harm is equally possible. An expert system is simply a computer program that has been fed (programmed with) data and information pertinent to its purpose.

If a medical doctor is faced with an ailing child who just returned from a vacation in Borneo, she might deduce that he is suffering from a tropical disease, one that is possibly infectious. Malaria or dengue fever are possibilities but she is not sure so she consults a program by inputting symptoms and the computer spews out possibilities. It does not sympathize with nor care about the patient nor the many people who may be infected; it does not lament the fact that living creatures suffer from bacterial and viral ailments; it does not consider the fate of the infected boy. It is an automated device that answers questions based on algorithms, in precisely the same way that Apple's Suri or IBM's Watson react to queries in what appears to be a conscious and rational manner.

Those who wish to be fooled by this simulacrum of reality will be. Others take a more balanced stance. If the infectious disease program is mistaken, does it lose its license to practice medicine? Can it be sued? Is it responsible for its waywardness? Of course not: It is an inanimate object that can compute, correlate, and discover. It is neither sentient nor conscious. Its programmers, not its binary code, are responsible for its successes and failures.

And it is madness to give expert systems the power to make final decisions concerning health benefits and payments but this often occurs: Medical personnel and the fate of their patients are controlled by algorithms! Mark Alfino discusses the moral costs of these systems which seem to obviate human judgment (16). This may be the case but it is possible (ethically mandated) to ignore their suggestions, which is exactly what should be done when a human being's life or death is being contemplated in terms of a cost benefit analysis.

Robotics

Robot ethics implies two very different possibilities. On the one hand we have the ethical application and use of robots, no small feat given the endless possibilities for employee displacement, dehumanization, and their purposeful misuse in human and inhumane activities such as the control or enslavement of people and the insinuation of robotic weaponry into conventional warfare so that drones decimate human armies and civilian populations. The second possibility is what concerns us here and that is the moral agency (ethical actions) of robots. But there are initial insurmountable problems: Not only do philosophers and neuroscientists claim that there is no such thing as free will for humans, based on specious reasoning—(a) every result must have a cause or (b) the brain makes decisions milliseconds prior to conscious choice (Crabtree)—but, impossibly, we are not conscious: "Are we really conscious? ... It sure seems like it. But brain science suggests we're not" (Graziano). Nevertheless, it is necessary to pursue roboethics as if we were.

No sane person would claim, one would hope, that a robotic arm, programmed to perform a simple repetitive task such as soldering a connector on a small chip board or welding a joint on a large car frame, is sentient or conscious, has the ability to think or feel emotions, is responsible, has agency let alone moral agency. Living human beings are denied agency, ethically and legally, if they are too young or too old, too ill or too demented. The criminally insane get away with murder, because they lack agency. We even distinguish a 17 year old from someone a year older who has reached his majority. Lawrence Kohlberg insists that moral sensitivity develops in stages as one grows ever older. The mature and healthy take over and control the destinies of those with little if any mental competence; those denied not only now lack agency, they have concomitantly lost their freedom, the single most important human right after the right to life itself. Of course, if we lack free will (and consciousness), one must logically conclude that we also lack agency.

So too, one would like to believe, no one would claim agency for a more complex, inanimate robotic *device* such as a Roomba vacuum cleaner, though apparently some folks become emotionally attached to it. Anki Cozmo Robot, a $180 child's toy, is artificially intelligent, "knows" its owner, and rolls around on treads. Were it to "purposely" run over a little girl and hurt her, would it be responsible? tried? convicted? go to jail? A robot is merely a self-driving automobile on wheels or treads or legs instead of tires, a mechanism, an entity with no consciousness or moral agency. A super computer such as Watson, which can beat humans at chess and *Jeopardy* is a powerful computer not a sentient *being;* it has no agency; a golden retriever has more and its agency is severely limited.

This is the single most bizarre development in the long history of Western ethics and indeed in the history of (serious) ideas (but see Waller's equally bizarre position in Chapter 3)—that manufactured devices may develop sentience and consciousness and therefore have (ethical) agency. Algorithmically self-driving cars simply follow protocols and make mistakes; when they kill a driver are they ethically culpable? are they punished? Here artificial intelligence (AI) practitioners get carried away with their hopes and dreams and the philosophically-minded theorize too broadly. Isaac Asimov's robot ethics is science fiction. Nevertheless, Carnegie Mellon plans to establish a center to study the ethics of AI (Markoff).

Some serious robot ethicists present grotesquely convoluted arguments to further their beliefs: they insist, for example, that noncognitive ethics (resulting in moral machines) is a possibility. Keith Abney claims that robots, though lacking emotions, could "be moral persons" because they may be able to deliberate rationally (47), but they also lack freedom to act otherwise, which seems to be a real impediment. So he adduces "quantum theories of consciousness" and quantum computing which lead to parallel universes and this somehow shows that robots have moral agency and are "full moral persons" (48, 50). If this convinces you, fine. I think it borders on madness.

On the other hand, even some committed robotics scholars agree with me: Matthias Scheutz insists that "Clearly, current robots (and those in the near future) will neither be self-governing agents that want to be autonomous, nor will they be in a position where they could be accountable or held accountable for their actions" (207). He admonishes that we must be careful about continuing to anthropomorphize social robots, which do not and cannot care about human beings. It is such a mistaken attitude that leads to the idea that mechanized devices have moral agency. They do not (215). Robots do not think, consider, desire, nor dream; they merely (re)act algorithmically, because they lack sentience and consciousness. Nevertheless, most roboethicists claim autonomy (and ethical) agency for their mechanical offspring.

18. Expert Systems, Robotics, War

Here is a slightly different take on roboethics. Johannes Marx and Christine Tiefensee agree that animals have rights but neither duties nor citizenship (83) and therefore they cannot have moral agency. And at the same time, they admit that "robots are inanimate automatons, not autonomous agents" and therefore currently "rights, duties, and citizenship" are not relevant (83); but in the future, more advanced devices will somehow transcend these boundaries (84). They also indicate that robots are intelligent, they learn, and therefore will not merely *simulate* conscious decision-making; in the future, they will actually be capable of making decisions (84). Therefore, they will have agency and, speculatively, moral agency. Indeed, "Robots might be right[s]-holders" (86) and "[F]uture robots could be interpreted as moral agents" (87) as well as actual citizens (88). It is devastatingly ironic that here we have the case of sentient, conscious, affective domestic animals being denied standing, which is then potentially allocated to mechanical, electronic, manufactured machines. We will cohabit with robots and blithely continue to eat beefsteak and lobster.

Making choices based on algorithms can never be the same as making ethical decisions based in *human* intelligence, knowledge, and experience but especially in understanding and predicting what not merely the immediate but the infinite number of future consequences may be, and not just for the situation at hand but for additional possibilities and ramifications. These are things that cannot be programmed into a mechanized device, but rather derive from a lifetime of experience and exist within a human being sometimes subconsciously. No computer will, ever be humanized nor will it be able to "understand" how Donald Trump fully differs from John F. Kennedy nor could it predict the untoward consequences of electing a demagogue to the presidency of the United States. Apparently, neither can we.

Even more extreme are Robin Hanson's contentions examined in great detail in a 400 page tome: *The Age of Em* (brain emulation) offers us a future inhabited by artificially intelligent entities that derive their power from scanned human brains (that thereby may transfer the minds and memories of a living human being into a computer program). Ems exist in robotic bodies but also in virtual reality. Hanson is serious about this and predicts it will occur within about a century (6, 8, 6). Readers may forgive the present author's skepticism especially since ethical matters are relegated to four succinct, passing comments on morality. Should such an unlikely possibility come to pass, despite obvious socially mandated ethical strictures against it, it might be feasible to imagine a manufactured robot with ethical agency, possible but highly improbable. This is a science fiction fantasy disguised as a scholarly study.

A similar, outlandish (grotesque) scenario predicates the physical intersection of a functioning human brain with a manufactured (metallic, plastic) algorithmically programed, autonomous robotic device. Here we are dealing not with a non-sentient robot, should this ever come to pass ethically, socially, and physically, but with a cyborg, a very different entity whose brain brings sentience along with it into its peculiar new being.

Wendell Wallach and Colin Allen, advocates for moral machines, rhetorically wonder whether "humanity really want[s] computers making morally important decisions" but they have decided for us and their answer, naturally, is yes (6). They take us to task by denigrating us: "It is easy to argue from a position of ignorance that the goal of artificial moral agency is impossible to achieve" (14). These prophets of doom recapitulate James Moor's hierarchy of artificial ethical agency (33–34), but the subtle distinctions do very little to negate the fact that computerized robots are reacting to protocols implanted through algorithmic coding. Nonbiological robots are not making ethical decisions because, as noted, they are neither conscious nor capable of thinking; and they are not ethically responsible for their reactions which may have positive or negative results in the real human world. Machine ethics is an oxymoron.

The December 2006 issue of *IRIE* covers "Ethics in Robotics" and *Ethics and Information Technology* offers two issues on the topic: December 2016 revolves around "Ethics and Social Robots" and September 2010 presents essays on "Robot Ethics and Human Ethics."

Conventional and Informational Warfare

If robotic agency is controversial, war is more so. Ethical (informational) warfare and a just war are oxymorons. It is never acceptable to sabotage or destroy another country's infrastructure or to kill another human being (or animal for that matter), which does not stop even Hindus and Buddhists (and perhaps Jains) from doing so in certain situations. *Hacksaw Ridge*, based on a true account, is an excellent cinematic example of how difficult it is to stand up for one's principles and defy common sense, logic, and cultural and social idiocies that have obtained and controlled human destiny since we first evolved from our primate ancestors: The soldier who refuses to carry a gun in battle saves more than 75 men; he won the Medal of Honor! Robotic warriors and machines are equally abhorrent unless they are just destroying each other, which is also disgusting. Humans should respect not only other people but also natural and artificial entities. The destructive instinct is humanity's greatest tragic flaw.

War is as much a part of humankind's heritage as is its quest for security, food, exploration, and intellectual progress. People fight against other people using weaponry, sometimes with enormous armies on even larger battlegrounds; but recently, things have diminished and terrorists "fight" smaller battles by killing themselves and their sisters and brothers, while the aggrieved fight back attempting to defend themselves and avert additional disaster. The wars in Korea or Vietnam were essentially different from the domestic and international war on terror, where the term war is used metaphorically, and the battles are not going well. Two simple solutions exist: Make peace with the enemy or make him pay such an outlandish price for his barbaric evils that he will stop of his own accord. But the enemy will not make peace and the West's general liberal attitude will not allow for the required unlimited vengeance. And so we move ahead into a bleak war-torn future.

Naturally, one may (should) defend oneself, one's kin, one's tribe, one's country from the onslaught of barbarians. War would long ago have been eliminated if megalomaniacs such as Alexander the Great, Genghis Khan, Napoleon, Stalin, Hitler, and innumerable other fanatics had not had greedy intentions or even legitimate complaints against their overseers. And naturally, too, warfare can be carried out in a more or less ethical manner, which means not immolating a fellow human being with a flamethrower, carpet bombing or napalming civilians, torturing people in concentration camps, or wantonly murdering them; these actions would be considered, by most decent people in any society at almost any time in history, to be unethical. It is evil to inculcate youngsters to the majesty of war through disgusting and violent films such as *Hunger Games*, wherein children kill their peers for an audience's entertainment, and which seems to be culturally acceptable, and video games such as *World of Warcraft, Mortal Kombat,* and *Halo,* which induce young boys and girls (and adults too) to waste hundreds of hours of their lives violently destroying when they should be creating or skiing or learning about and enjoying nature (even urban areas have parks and natural habitats). Nobody cares. The worst case scenario for future physical warfare is drones and robots programmed (with "agency"!) to "kill" not other machines but rather human beings. What a monstrous development.

It is possible to act unethically within traditional warfare. This is why Christopher Coker insists that "ethical practices ... inhere in the nature of war itself." Ethical commitment is not a mere addition, but rather lies at the very center "of military operations" (x); it derives not from "laws and conventions" but rather from the honor of warriors (14). Nevertheless, "ethical rules help society win wars... (16). "Etiquettes of atrocity," that is, "laws of war" (20), change over time, but it has always been unethical to kill civilians, though this inadvertently occurs even today, and most older adults will have little trouble recalling the purposeful My Lai murders, one of many heinous massacres in but one of many barbaric wars.

If data and information are and always have been crucial for conventional warfare, they are the raison d'être for seeking or destroying in cyberspace, where personal, corporate, or governmental espionage and hacking lead to success, and failure to discover secrets or to attempt to cripple an enemy's electric grid may prove as disastrous as losing a conventional land, sea, or air battle. In information warfare no one is harmed or killed directly as in bombing or machine gunning; rather, the stolen data and information, the alteration in an automobile's or electric or gas company's or air traffic controller's operations have a secondary effect that may indeed prove fatal—for the driver, the freezing widow, or the plane's passengers.

In 2008, Greta E. Marlatt compiled *Information Warfare and Information Operations (IW/IO): A Bibliography,* a 335 page document (https://www.hsdl.org/?view&did=443229). Information warfare is big business. The December 2013 issue of *IRIE* is devoted to cyber warfare and the June 2013 number of *Ethics and Information Technology* has as its theme "Armed Military Robots."

19   Images, Imaging
and the Imagination

When one thinks of images, photography, naturally, comes to mind and especially now when almost everyone who acquires a smart phone seems to think that clicking its shutter results in photos worth preserving. Much worse are the millions of superfluous images created in order to send a textual Snapchat message. What a burden on the universe! But images also include nonphotographic artwork, illustrations, and scans from many sources including X-rays, magnetic resonance imaging (MRI), and computer axial tomography (CAT). The use and application of any of these systems can result in abusive, unethical manipulation or misinterpretation.

Anyone who has ever worked in a darkroom knows that enlarging, cropping, dodging, and burning are all necessary adjuncts to printing an excellent photo. Even leaving a print in the developer for a shorter or longer time will alter the tonal quality of the image. Here there may be no intention to manipulate or deceive. Digital alterations are even easier to accomplish now: With advanced versions of Photoshop, an amateur can produce whatever he or she desires, and even an expert may not be able to detect alterations. At times, the result is just a better photo. But when the intention is to deceive, especially if a contest, for example, calls for unaltered images, then the action is unethical.

The history of manipulated photographs stretches all the way back to Mathew Brady, who presumably set up American Civil War scenes as did Robert Capa, the photographer of "Falling Soldier," the famous Spanish Civil War image. Even the flag raising on Iwo Jima has been considered staged. All three of these are merely historical documentations. They may not be as transgressive as creating a false photo whose aim is to cause harm, though some people would probably disagree. There are, however, a number of ways in which digital images can be secured and authenticated, including "watermarking, image headers, encryption, authentication protocols, and password protection" (Rockenbach 67).

The legal rights of publicly photographed subjects are nonexistent but ethical considerations could help to control abuse. It is shameful that the law is so uncaringly absolutist so that if a precedent indicates it is acceptable to take a picture of a naked woman through her shadeless window and publish it, that is okay; she is a *public* spectacle. Ethically, it is an inconsiderate abomination. Even less protected are archival materials: In a remarkable article, Suzannah Biernoff discusses the misuse of appropriated images of injured First World War military personnel for the titillation of players of *BioShock,* a game offered to the public in 2007. The images depict men with horribly disfigured facial features and using them in the game is disrespectful of their dignity, pain, and suffering. In some cases the viewer would be incapable of even looking at them. It is an invasion of the privacy of these long-dead men to *use* their representations even in a museum exhibit, let alone in a violent video game. Respect for the dead (and the living) is much lacking in contemporary society.

Photography also produces theoretical constructs, some of which are misleading or false; this is especially a problem when it comes to postmodernist theoretical applications that are often in jargon-infested articulations that may defy comprehension. If one were to look out of a window and see a field, some trees, and a rambling brook, that is what is there. The scene has no allusive, semiotic, interpretive, or mythic meaning. It just is. If a person (or worse, an automated camera that clicks once an hour) takes a photograph of the scene, it is somehow ostensibly imbued with all kinds of exquisitely meaningful overtones. This is absurd. Not every image leads to Nirvana. This author's 15 year old daughter takes 140 arbitrarily chosen photos throughout each day in order to communicate on Snapchat. The results do not engage with the following:

> It should be clarified, as Victor Burguin and W. J. T. Mitchell explain, that every photograph signifies on the basis of a plurality of codes and that a photograph's privileged relation to language causes its image to function as a kind of text. The photograph is a mechanism that allows us to see and to speak out of a

heterogenous array of discourses that together constitute what Gilles Deleuze refers to as the "curves of visibility and the curves of enunciation." In the same way, the relation between the image and verbal discourse must be understood as simultaneous and dialectical. This relation is manifest in what Mitchell refers to as the "pictorial turn" in contemporary culture, with the postlinguistic, postsemiotic discovery of painting in an interwoven complex of visuality, discourses, institutions, disciplinary apparatuses, bodies, and figuration [González-Stephan 26].

There is more but this is enough to indicate that postmodernist thought processes and articulation are informationally misleading as well as intellectually incomprehensible. In this case, they are also patently false, no matter how many scholars (including respected thinkers such as Mitchell) and esoteric terms are squeezed into a single brief paragraph. They do not help nor elucidate. They merely confuse.

Another problem that derives from media photographers and videographers is the use of certain images that perpetrate stereotypes. This is a diabolical dilemma because the articulation of newsworthy events may concentrate on or demand material concerning certain countries, religions, ethnicities, sexes, illnesses, or even natural disasters all of which may emphasize something that leads to stereotypical misdirection. A simple example of an arcane possibility is the Zika virus, but in Brazil, or the contention that because women are physically weaker they therefore cannot accomplish what men can.

To be of evidentiary usage, medical images require a skilled interpreter. Anyone can see spots on a lung or a bad fracture on a bone X-ray, but subtle differences on soft surfaces represented on an MRI scan may mean many things. Not being scrupulous in examining and evaluating what is seen is an ethical breach, one that might result in death and therefore a civil suit. Doctors, in this case, radiologists, make mistakes and that is why malpractice insurance is expensive; sometimes the rates are quite reasonable, depending on one's location, but they also can run to $61,000 and as high as $187,000 per year. (It now appears that computers do a better job than radiologists at spotting problems.)

Manipulation is a well-known aspect of image reproduction. To fail to suspect that the imagination has been at work when viewing any image or cinematic reproduction is to be naive in the extreme. During the past half century or so, whenever a purported visual recording was introduced into judicial proceedings as evidence, the protagonists or the court might call upon an expert witness who could confirm that the film or tape was an original, undoctored representation of what occurred. But sometimes all that was required was for someone to affirm under oath that the material was unaltered. If a person is willing to submit false evidence, it is doubtful that he or she would mind committing perjury. Images and recordings are unreliable, and biological scientists accompany their submitted papers with doctored images that more fully confirm their claims. Even the sophisticated and knowledgeable can be taken in by agenda-driven film directors like Oliver Stone who sprinkle reality with false or misleading conspiratorial nonsense in, for example, his *JFK* (1991) and more recent *Snowden* (2016), just two of his 25 films (not including those he produced).

William J. Mitchell in *The Reconfigured Eye,* his early seminal study, notes that "image truth, authenticity, and originality" have become ethically and legally problematic, and he thinks that traditional standards are now inadequate to deal with the new challenges (52) (a perhaps misguided perspective that we have encountered before in relation to ethical decision-making). The various copyright and other rights problems he discusses are difficult and may appear insoluble. Thus, he insists that "the digital image is emerging as a new kind of token—differing fundamentally from both photographs and paintings—in communicative and economic exchanges. It demands new rules for structuring those exchanges" (55).

It is natural that a new technology, especially one as far-reaching as digital manipulation of new and older (digitized) materials, creates contingent situations through duplication, alteration, coloration, or theft, but appropriate ethical and legal mandates do exist, the most important being caring consideration for other people and their property and rights. Lamentably, this does not work well in the real world, and that is why additional and more complex laws are passed, which have a controlling and deadening effect, but which also fail to stem the burgeoning tide of image usurpation.

Conclusion

Information ethics is a burgeoning field because bad things happen and human beings seem incapable of acting as they should without some guidance. At times, this is understandable, since diametrically opposed necessities compete with each other and it is difficult to know what one should do. Additionally, personal and professional demands may conflict (in information work, academics, research, police protection, medicine, law) and there may be no correct solution to an appalling dilemma. A most unpleasant example is abortion: the government should not control women, their bodies, and how they react to circumstances, but since abortion is murder, even a woman contemplating such a procedure and for good legitimate reasons, must give pause, if she considers the consequences. This may be an especially difficult decision for a medical practitioner asked to participate. Ethical decisions concerning information play a decisive role when the law is unavailable to help, guide, or control.

These practical considerations are now undergirded by some theoretical conjecturing on the part especially of Capurro and Floridi, whose extensive publication and public lecture records lend credence to IE's more practical implementations, which the preceding chapters have made patently clear.

Information ethics long ago crossed the boundary separating scholarly rumination and theorizing to invade the popular imagination. Eventually, one hopes, we will all awake. Many people read in hard copy and online but not necessarily work that emphasizes IE. Many more, however, are privy to IE problems through film, which they view when one is well-received and they are lured to the theater (or Netflix). The concept of information ethics is thereby disseminated widely, although most layper-

Conclusion

sons are unconscious of it except as exemplified in a popular work. Ethical situations, problems, or dilemmas have always provided scholars and novelists and especially both Hollywood and documentary film makers with content. One thinks of *All the King's Men* and *Gandhi* or Frederick Wiseman's overpowering *Titicut Follies* and *Domestic Violence* and the work of Roger Moore, e.g., *Fahrenheit 9/11* or *Bowling for Columbine*. But as information has taken precedence over agriculture, manufacturing, and other societal necessities, more pointed cinema dealing precisely with information ethics—the misuse or abuse of information—has emerged. Extraordinary works include Orwell's prescient *1984* (various versions), *Ace in the Hole*, *All the President's Men*, *WarGames*, *Sneakers*, *The Net*, *Hackers*, *Disclosure*, *Broken Glass*, *Inception*, *AI Artificial Intelligence*, *The Social Network*, *The Imitation Game*, *Sully*, *Denial*, *The Witness*, *Author*, *Lo and Behold: Reveries of the Connected World*, *The Fifth Estate*, *We Steal Secrets: The Story of WikiLeaks*, *We Are Legion*, and *Salinger* among many other possibilities.

Film directors sometimes distort or pervert the truth in order to achieve some higher end and this is manifested in *Selma*, *The Imitation Game*, and *Citizenfour*, among other recent works.

For those who keep up with global news, IE also manifests itself in financial and political crises ranging from the mendacity of many politicians to the Wells Fargo debacle, Russia's disinformation program, and the Manning and Snowdon revelations. It seems as if we have reached a point at which the wrong information misapplied could have a most devastating effect on humankind and the physical world. Be wary, be informed, and be safe!

Afterword

by Elizabeth A. Buchanan

Walking away from Robert Hauptman's *The Scope of Information Ethics* leaves one anxious and exhausted. This is a good thing. Psychological, physical, moral anxiety and exhaustion are needed in one's life, to escape the shackles of everyday rituals. Hauptman was determined to push his readers, to push all of us, to the edges, to force us to think about choices we all make every day. Hauptman wants us to see the dark and ugly sides, the unethical sides, of "information." And, why would anyone expect less of this seminal figure, this provocative, dedicated author and scholar?

I have known Robert Hauptman for over twenty years, and he has never compromised his values; this work reminded me of this clearly. As I read through this encyclopedic overview of information ethics, I was reminded of his early work, which I first encountered while completing my master's degree in library and information studies. Having come from a philosophy undergraduate degree, I engaged immediately with Hauptman's thoughts; he was then a practicing librarian but spoke as an ethicist. He brought to light the complexities of a field, a profession, a discipline; he made people think beyond the surface.

As with all of Hauptman's publications, the present work covers the widest and broadest array of topics, all of which are stitched together through the thread of "information ethics." What started as an intellectual and professional exercise, I think, for Hauptman became inseparable from how individuals choose to live their lives. There is no separation from the personal and professional, for him. The detailed intricacies of society, technology, science, business, agriculture, and so on, are ultimately

Afterword by Elizabeth Buchanan

interconnected, and ignoring this fact is both symptom and symptomatic of the forces Hauptman critiques so vehemently. WAKE UP, he says. This is not a simple academic treatise, but a manifesto.

The Scope of Information Ethics is unlike most academic writing. It is beyond scholarship: it is not strictly from a discipline, nor is it limited to any discipline. It is simultaneously autobiographical, critical, historical, social, mythical, in addition to philosophical. Will philosophical purists like this work? Will present-day scholars in the field of information ethics embrace it? Will some simply detest the work for what it brings to light? And where will this work lead us? What is its goal?

I believe this work provides a window into Hauptman's intellect and his lifelong pursuit in information ethics. From the anecdotes of his childhood, his home, and his reflections on food and medications, I am left thinking about others whose writings exhausted me, and yet left me thinking of begging for social change; other writers, who have written about the interconnectedness of it all, those who looked back, historically while surveying the present, and envisioning our futures.

I cannot imagine what Robert Hauptman will write next, but, with anxiety and exhaustion, I do look forward to it.

Elizabeth A. Buchanan, Ph.D., holds the endowed chair in ethics at the University of Wisconsin–Stout.

Bibliography

The following replete bibliography also contains a limited number of entries for some of the influential authors or studies merely mentioned in passing in the text as well as the titles of germane journals. There are a group of prolific scholars (including Rafael Capurro, Charles Ess, Luciano Floridi, Richard Spinello, and Herman Tavani) who concentrate specifically on IE and a few though not all of their many works appear below. This bibliography functions as a fairly comprehensive listing of both theoretical and practical aspects of information ethics, though readers should be aware that that there exists an enormous body of work on many of the subjects covered in this study and only some of this is included here.

Abney, Keith. "Robotics, Ethical Theory, and Metaethics: A Guide for the Perplexed." In *Robot Ethics: The Ethical and Social Implications of Robotics*, edited by Patrick Lin, Keith Abney, and George A. Bekey. Cambridge, MA: MIT Press, 2012: 35–52.

Accountability in Research, 1989–.

AIA. *2017 Code of Ethics and Professional Conduct*. http://aiad8.prod.acquia-sites.com/sites/default/files/2017-08/2017%20Code%20Update.pdf

Alfino, Mark. "Do Expert Systems Have a Moral Cost?" *Journal of Information Ethics*, 2.2 (Fall 1993): 15–19.

Angulo, A. J. "Ignorance." *Miseducation: A History of Ignorance-Making in America and Abroad*, edited by A. J. Angulo. Baltimore: Johns Hopkins University Press, 2016, pp. 1–10.

_____. "Reflections." *Miseducation: A History of Ignorance-Making in America and Abroad*, edited by A. J. Angulo. Baltimore: Johns Hopkins University Press, 2016, pp. 339–350.

Angulo, A. J., ed. *Miseducation: A History of Ignorance-Making in America and Abroad*. Baltimore: Johns Hopkins University Press, 2016.

Aristotle. *Nicomachean Ethics*. David Ross, trans. Oxford World's Classics 1998. Oxford, UK: Oxford University Press, 1925.

Bibliography

Ash, Timothy Garton. *Free Speech: Ten Principles for a Connected World*. New Haven: Yale University Press, 2016.

Author: The JT LeRoy Story. [Film]. Dir. Jeff Feurzeig. A&E IndieFilms, 2016.

Baird, Julia. "Victoria's Secrets." *The New York Times*, 20 November 2016: 8 SR.

Bartlett, Tom. "Power Poser: When Big Ideas Go Bad." *The Chronicle of Higher Education*, 9 December 2016: B4–B7.

Bartoli, Alberto, and Eric Medvet. "Bibliometric Evaluation of Researchers in the Internet Age." *The Information Society*, 30.5 (2014). http://www.indiana.edu/~tisj/30/5/ab-bartoli.html

Basken, Paul. "As Concerns Grow About Using Data to Measure Faculty Members, a Company Changes Its Message." *The Chronicle of Higher Education*, 21 October 2016: A14.

Bielby, Jared. "Information Ethics I: Origins and Evolutions." 2014. https://www.linkedin.com/pulse/20140625225908-299816747-information-ethics-i-origins-and-evolutions [also http://icie.zkm.de/research]

———. "Information Ethics II: Towards a Unified Taxonomy." 2014. https://www.linkedin.com/pulse/20140625225838-299816747-information-ethics-i-origins-and-evolutions [also http://icie.zkm.de/research]

Biernoff, Suzannah. "Medical Archives and Digital Culture." *Photographies*, 5.2 (September 2012): 179–202. https://www.ncbi.nlm.nih.gov/pmc/articles/PMC4851239/

"The Big Religion Chart: Comparison Chart." http://www.religionfacts.com/http://www.religionfacts.com/big-religion-chart

Bloche, M. Gregg. "When Doctors First Do Harm." *The New York Times*, 23 November 2016: A25.

Bohannon, John. "Who's Afraid of Peer Review?" *Science* (342, 6154), 4 October 2013: 60–65. http://science.sciencemag.org/content/342/6154/60.full

Brey, Philip. "Is Information Ethics Culture-Relative?" *International Journal of Technology and Human Interaction*, 3.3 (July/September 2007): 12–24. http://www.igi-global.com/article/information-ethics-culture-relative/2904 [Abstract only.]

Britz, Johannes, Peter Lor and Theo Bothma. "Global Capitalism and the Fair Distribution of Information in the Marketplace: A Moral Reflection from the Perspective of the Developing World." *Journal of Information Ethics*, 15.1 (Spring 2006): 60–69.

Broad, William, and Nicholas Wade. *Betrayers of the Truth: Fraud and Deceit in the Halls of Science*. New York: Simon & Schuster, 1982.

Buchanan, Elizabeth, ed. *Readings in Virtual Research Ethics: Issues and Controversies*. Hershey, PA: Idea Group, 2004.

Cabranes, José A. "The New 'Surveillance University'." *The Washington Post Weekly*, 15 January 2017: Opinions.

Capurro, Rafael. "On Floridi's Metaphysical Foundation of Information Ecology," ca. 2008. http://www.capurro.de/floridi.html

———. "Towards an Ontological Foundation of Information Ethics." 2005. http://www.capurro.de/oxford.html

Bibliography

Carbo, Toni, and Martha M. Smith. "Global Information Ethics: Intercultural Perspectives on Past and Future Research." *Journal of the American Society for Information Science and Technology*, 59.7 (2008): 1111–1123.

Cohen, I. Glenn, and Holly Fernandez Lynch (eds.). *Human Subjects Research Regulation: Perspectives on the Future*. Cambridge, MA: MIT Press, 2014.

Coker, Christopher. *Ethics and War in the 21st Century*. London: Routledge, 2008.

Cornog, Martha. "Erotophobia, Homophobia, and Censorship in U.S. Libraries: An Historical Overview." *Journal of Information Ethics*, 25.2 (Fall 2016): 42–58.

Cox, Richard J. "Testing the Spirit of the Information Age." *Journal of Information Ethics*, 10.2 (Fall 2001): 51–66.

Crabtree, Vexen. "The Illusion of Choice: Free Will and Determinism." *Science and Truth Versus Mass Confusion*. 1999. http://www.humantruth.info/free_will.html

DeGrazia, Edward. *Girls Lean Back Everywhere: The Law of Obscenity and the Assault on Genius*. New York: Random House, 1992.

Denial. [Film]. Dir. Mick Jackson. London: BBC Films, 2106.

Donadio, Rachel, and Jennifer Schuessler. "Supporters of Ferrante Are Irritated by Exposé." *The New York Times*, 5 October 2016: C1, C6.

Doty, Philip. "Ethics, Risk and U.S. Government Secrecy." *Journal of Information Ethics*, 24.1 (Spring 2015): 11–47.

Doyle, Tony. "A Critique of Information Ethics." *Knowledge, Technology & Policy*, 23.1, 2 (2010): 163–175.

_____. "MacKinnon on Pornography." *Journal of Information Ethics*, 11.2 (Fall 2002): 53–78.

Dreid, Nadia. "Meet the Professor Who's Calling Out Clickbait." *The Chronicle of Higher Education*, 2 December 2016: A24.

Du, Susan. "No Worries, Mr. Pedophile." *City Pages*, 21–27 December 2016: 5.

Duff, Alastair S. *A Normative Theory of the Information Society*. New York: Routledge, 2012.

_____. "Contra Bentham: Ethical Information Policy in the PanopticEon." *Journal of Information Ethics*, 26.1 (Spring 2017): 93–111.

Ehrenreich, Barbara. *Nickel and Dimed: On (Not) Getting By in America*. New York: Henry Holt, 2002.

Epstein, William M. "The Lighter Side of Deception Research in the Social Sciences: Social Work as Comedy." *Journal of Information Ethics*, 15.1 (Spring 2006): 11–26.

Ess, Charles. *Digital Media Ethics*. (2nd ed.) Cambridge, UK: Polity Press, 2014.

"Ethical Aspects of Book Reviewing." *Journal of Information Ethics*, 11.1 (Spring 2002): entire issue.

Ethics & Behavior, 1991–.

Etzioni, Amitai. "The First Amendment Is Not an Absolute Even on the Internet." *The Journal of Information Ethics*, 6.2 (Fall 1997): 64–66.

"First Amendment Rights." *The Journal of Information Ethics*, 6.2 (Fall 1997): entire issue.

Bibliography

"Five Biggest Engineering Disasters." Engineering.com 11 February 2013. https://www.engineering.com/Library/ArticlesPage/tabid/85/ArticleID/5301/Five-Biggest-Engineering-Disasters.aspx

Floridi, Luciano. *The Ethics of Information.* Oxford, UK: Oxford University Press, 2013.

Forrester, Katrina. "Lights. Camera. Action. Making Sense of Modern Pornography." *The New Yorker,* 26 September 2016: 64–68.

Foucault, Michel. *Discipline and Punish: The Birth of the Prison.* New York: Pantheon, 1977.

Froehlich, Thomas. "A Brief History of Information Ethics." *BiD: textos universitaris de biblioteconomia i documentació,* 13 December 2004. http://bid.ub.edu/13froel2.htm

Geffert, Bryn. "Piracy Fills a Publishing Need." *The Chronicle of Higher Education,* 9 September 2016: B4–B5.

Gettleman, Jeffrey. "Evidence of Graft Paints Congo's Leader Into a Corner as His Term Ends." *The New York Times,* 18 December 2016: 6Y, Y17.

Glanz, James, Gaia Pianigiani, Jeremy White, and Karthik Patanjali. "Hanging by a Thread: Behind a Bridge Collapse." *The New York Times,* 7 September 2018: A1, A6–A7.

Gleick, James. *The Information: A History, a Theory, a Flood.* New York: Pantheon, 2011.

Goel, Vindu. "Selling Ads on Fake Sites, Russian Ring Steals Up to $5 Million Daily." *The New York Times,* 21 December 2016: B1, B3.

Goitein, Elizabeth. "Secret Law Is Bad Law." *The New York Times,* 18 October 2016: A21.

González-Stephan, Beatriz. "The Dark Side of Photography: Techno-Aesthetics, Bodies, and the Residues of Coloniality in Nineteenth-Century Latin America." *Discourse,* 38.1 (Winter 2016): 22–45.

Grabosky, P.N., and Russell G. Smith. "Digital Crime in the Twenty-First Century." *Journal of Information Ethics,* 10.1 (Spring 2001): 8–26.

Graziano, Michael S. A. "Are We Really Conscious?" *The New York Times,* 12 October 2014: 12 SR.

Guterman, Lila. "Hot Type: Kiss and Disclose." *The Chronicle of Higher Education,* 6 December 2002: A18.

Hamilton, Richard F. *The Social Misconstruction of Reality: Validity and Verification in the Scholarly Community.* New Haven, CT: Yale University Press, 1996.

Han, Byung-Chul. *In the Swarm: Digital Prospects.* Tr. Erik Butler. Cambridge, MA: MIT Press, 2017. (Catalogue.) https://mitpress.mit.edu/books/swarm

Hanson, Robin. *The Age of Em: Work, Love, and Life When Robots Rule the Earth.* New York: Oxford University Press, 2016.

Hartemann, Frederic V., and Robert Hauptman. *Deadly Peaks: Mountaineering's Greatest Triumphs and Tragedies.* Guilford, CT: Falcon Guides, 2016.

Hauptman, Robert. *Authorial Ethics: How Writers Abuse Their Calling.* Lanham, MD: Lexington Books, 2011.

_____. *Documentation: A History and Critique of Attribution, Commentary, Glosses,*

Bibliography

Marginalia, Notes, Bibliographies, Works-Cited Lists, and Citation Indexing and Analysis. Jefferson, NC: McFarland, 2008.

———. *Ethical Challenges in Librarianship.* Phoenix, AZ: Oryx, 1988.

———. "Ethics: Casuistry, Conscience, Convenience." *Crisis Magazine,* 1 June 1983. http://www.crisismagazine.com/1983/ethics-casuistry-conscience-convenience

———. "Professionalism or Culpability? An Experiment in Ethics." Wilson Library Bulletin, 50 (April 1976): 626–627.

———. Review of *Against Moral Responsibility* by Bruce N. Waller. *Journal of Information Ethics,* 26.2 (Fall 2017): 128–132.

Head, Simon. *Mindless: Why Smarter Machines Are Making Dumber Humans.* New York: Basic Books, 2014.

Helfand, David J. *A Survival Guide to the Misinformation Age: Scientific Habits of Mind.* New York: Columbia University Press, 2016.

Hentoff, Nat. *Free Speech for Me But Not for Thee: How the American Left and Right Relentlessly Censor Each Other.* New York: HarperCollins, 1992.

Hess, Amanda. "The Latest Celebrity Diet? Cyberbullying." *The New York Times,* 13 October 2016: C1, C4.

Horrobin, David F. "Something Rotten at the Core of Science." http://stop-metha done.com/pdf/Something_Rotten_Horrobin.pdf

Huff, Darrell. *How to Lie with Statistics.* New York: W. W. Norton, 1954.

Information Society, 1981–.

Intellectual Freedom Manual. Eds. Trini Magi et al. 9th edition. Chicago: ALA, 2015.

International Journal of Technoethics, 2010–.

International Review of Information Ethics, 2004–.

Ioannidis, John P. A. "Why Most Published Research Findings Are False." *PLoS Medicine,* 30 August 2005. http://journals.plos.org/plosmedicine/article?id=10. 1371/journal.pmed.0020124

Israel, Howard. "The Nazi Origins of Eduard Pernkopf's *Topographische Anatomie des Menschen:* The Biomedical Ethical Issues." In *The Holocaust: Memories, Research, Reference,* eds. Robert Hauptman and Susan Hubbs Motin. New York: Haworth, 1998: 131–146.

Israel, Lee. *Can You Ever Forgive Me? Memoirs of a Literary Forger.* New York: Simon & Schuster, 2008.

Jackson, Ben. "Just About Anything You Want." Review of *The Boy Who Could Change the World* by Aaron Swartz. *London Review of Books,* 6 October 2016: 19–22.

Jenkins, Holman W., Jr. "After Nice, Fight Back with Better Spying." *The Wall Street Journal,* 16–17 July 2016: A13.

Johnson, David R., and E. H. Ecklund. "Ethical Ambiguity in Science." *Science and Engineering Ethics,* 22.4 (2016): 989–1005. (Abstract). http://link.springer.com/ article/10.1007/s11948-015-9682-9

Johnson, Deborah G. "Reframing the Question of Forbidden Knowledge for Modern Science." *Science and Engineering Ethics,* 5.4 (1999): 445–461. (Abstract). http:// link.springer.com/article/10.1007/s11948-999-0045-2

Bibliography

_____. *Computer Ethics*. 3rd ed. Upper Saddle River, NJ: Prentice Hall, 2001.

Jones, Meg Leta. *Ctrl + Z: The Right to Be Forgotten*. New York: New York University Press, 2016.

Journal of Information, Communication and Ethics in Society, 2003–.

Journal of Information Ethics, 1992–.

Kakutani, Michiko. "Ignorance As Bliss." Review of *The Death of Expertise: The Campaign Against Established Knowledge and Why It Matters* by Tom Nichols (New York: Oxford University Press, 2017). *The New York Times*, 22 March 2017: C1, C6.

Kant, Immanuel. *The Metaphysics of Morals*. trans. and ed. Mary Gregor. New York: Cambridge University Press, 1996.

Karasz, Palko. "Columbia Bridge Collapse Throws Workers to Their Deaths." *The New York Times*, 16 January 2018. https://www.nytimes.com/2018/01/16/world/americas/colombia-bridge-collapse.html

Klein, Marty. "Free Internet Porn and America: A Report on a Natural Experiment." *Free Inquiry*, 37.1 (December 2016/January 2017): 22–27.

Kramer, Andrew E. "Yet Another Russian Deception, Full of Hot Air." *The New York Times*, 13 October 2016: A1, A9.

Kronhausen, Phyllis, and Eberhard. *Pornography and the Law*. New York: Ballantine Books, 1959.

LaFollette, Marcel C. *Stealing into Print: Fraud, Plagiarism, and Misconduct in Scientific Publishing*. Berkeley: University of California Press, 1992.

Le, Vu. "Weaponized data: How the obsession with data has been hurting marginalized communities." (Blog post.) *Nonprofit with Balls*, 2015. http://nonprofit withballs.com/2015/05/weaponized-data-how-the-obsession-with-data-has-been-hurting-marginalized-communities/

LearnTechLib. https://www.learntechlib.org/search/?q=%22information+ethics%22.

Lee, Jasmine C., and Kevin Quealy. "All the People, Places and Things Donald Trump Has Insulted...." *The New York Times*, 24 October 2016: A10–A11.

Leiter, Brian. "Academic Ethics: What Should We Do with Sexual Harassers?" *The Chronicle of Higher Education*, 14 October 2016: A25.

Levitin, Daniel J. *A Field Guide to Lies: Critical Thinking in the Information Age*. New York: Dutton, 2016.

Lindner, Robert Mitchell. *The Fifty-Minute Hour: A Collection of True Psychoanalytic Tales*. New York: Rinehart, 1955.

Lipinski, Tomas A., and Elizabeth A. Buchanan. "The Impact of Copyright Law and Other Ownership Mechanisms on the Freedom of Inquiry: Infringements on the Public Domain." *Journal of Information Ethics*, 15.1 (Spring 2006): 47–59.

Lipstadt, Deborah. *Denying the Holocaust: The Growing Assault on Truth and Memory*. New York: The Free Press, 1993.

Liptak, Adam. "Trump Would Have Trouble Winning a Suit Over a Tax Article, Experts Say." *The New York Times*, 5 October 2016: A14.

Lucas, Edward. *Cyberphobia: Identity, Trust, Security and the Internet*. New York: Bloomsbury, 2015.

Bibliography

Lynch, Joe. "8 Songs Accused of Plagiarism That Hit No. 1 on the Billboard Hot 100 billboard." *Billboard*, 12 March 2015. http://www.billboard.com/articles/news/list/6501950/songs-accused-plagiarism-no-1-hot-100-blurred-lines

MacKinnon, Catharine A. *Only Words*. Cambridge, MA: Harvard University Press, 1993.

MacNeil, Heather. *Without Consent: The Ethics of Disclosing Personal Information in Public Archives*. Chicago: Society of American Archivists and Metuchen, NJ: Scarecrow Press, 1992.

Mallon, Thomas. *Stolen Words: Forays into the Origins and Ravages of Plagiarism*. New York: Ticknor & Fields, 1989.

Manjoo, Farhad. "As Internet Seizes News, Grip on Truth Loosens." *The New York Times*, 3 November 2016: B1, B7.

Maret, Susan. "Intellectual Freedom and U.S. Government Secrecy." *The Library Juice Press Handbook of Intellectual Freedom: Concepts, Cases, and Theories*, edited by Mark Alfino and Laura Koltusky. Sacramento, CA: Library Juice Press, 2014: 247–281.

Markham, Annette, and Elizabeth Buchanan. "Ethical Decision-Making and Internet Research: Recommendations from the AoIR Ethics Working Committee (Version 2.0)." Aoir, 2012. http://aoir.org/wp-content/uploads/2014/04/ethics2.pdf

Markoff, John. "New Research Center to Explore Ethics of Artificial Intelligence." *The New York Times*, 2 November 2016: B2.

Marks, Jonathan. "Coddled on Campus." Review of *Campus Politics* by Jonathan Zimmerman. *The Wall Street Journal*, 13 September 2016: A9.

Martin, Brian. "Correcting Errors: Strategic Considerations." *Journal of Information Ethics*, 24.2 (Fall 2015): 31–42.

Marx, Gary T. "Ethics for the New Surveillance." *The Information Society* 14 (1998): 171–185.

_____. *Windows into the Soul: Surveillance and Society in an Age of High Technology*. Chicago: University of Chicago Press, 2016.

Marx, Johannes, and Christine Tiefensee. "Of Animals, Robots and Men." *Historical Social Research/Historische Sozialforschung*, 40.4 (2015): 70–91. http://www.jstor.org/stable/24583247

Mashberg, Tom. "Antiquities Dealer Accused of Selling Stolen Artifacts." *The New York Times*, 22 December 2016: A25.

Mathiesen, Kay. "What Is Information Ethics?" *ACM SIGCAS Computers and Society*, 34.1 (June 2004).

Mazzei, Patricia. "A Crack Was Noted and Called No Hazard." *The New York Times*, 18 March 2018: Y 19.

Mazzei, Patricia, Nick Madigan, and Anemona Hartocollis. "Bridge Falls on Bustling Street: 'I Don't Know What Is Underneath.'" *The New York Times*, 16 March 2018: A13.

McIntyre, Lee. *Respecting Truth: Willful Ignorance in the Internet Age*. New York: Routledge, 2015.

Menand, Louis. "People of the Book." *The New Yorker*, 12 December 2016: ca. 78–85.

Bibliography

Milgram, Stanley. *Obedience to Authority: An Experimental View*. New York: Harper & Row, [1974].

Milligan, Ian. "The Problem of History in the Age of Abundance." *The Chronicle of Higher Education*, 16 December 2016: B4–B5.

Mitchell, William J. *The Reconfigured Eye: Visual Truth in the Post-Photographic Era*. Cambridge, MA: MIT Press, 2001 (1992).

Monahan, Torin. "Built to Lie: Investigating Technologies of Deception, Surveillance, and Control." *The Information Society*, 32.4 (2016): 229–240. http://publicsur veillance.com/papers/Built-to-lie.pdf

Monmonier, Mark. *How to Lie with Maps*. Chicago: University of Chicago Press, 1991.

Moore, Adam D., ed. *Information Ethics: Privacy, Property, and Power*. Seattle: University of Washington Press, 2005.

Moore, Nolan. "Ten Crazy Literary Conspiracy Theories." *Listverse* 27 October 2013. http://listverse.com/2013/10/27/10-crazy-literary-conspiracy-theories/

Moran, Gordon. *Silencing Scientists and Scholars in Other Fields: Power, Paradigm Controls, Peer Review, and Scholarly Communication*. Greenwich, CT: Ablex, 1998.

Morgan, Elizabeth. *The Making of a Woman Surgeon*. New York: G.P. Putnam's Sons, 1980.

Morozov, Evgeny. *The Net Delusion: The Dark Side of Internet Freedom*. New York: PublicAffairs, 2011.

Mozur, Paul, and Mark Scott. "Power for the Globe's Gullible: Facebook's Fake News Problem." *The New York Times*, 18 November 2016: A1, B4.

Nader, Ralph. *Unsafe at Any Speed: The Designed-in Dangers of the American Automobile*. New York: Grossman, 1965.

Neuroethics, 2008–.

The New York Times. "No Kegs, No Liquor: Colleges Crack Down." *The New York Times*, 30 October 2016: 14Y, 16Y.

Niebuhr, Reinhold, *Moral Man and Immoral Society: A Study in Ethics and Politics*. New York: Scribner's, 1932.

Nissenbaum, Helen. *Privacy in Context: Technology, Policy, and the Integrity of Social Life*. Stanford, CA: Stanford University Press, 2010.

Noble, Safiya U. *Algorithms of Oppression: How Search Engines Reinforce Racism*. New York: New York University Press, 2018.

O'Donohue, William, Cassandra Snipes, Georgia Dalto, Cyndy Soto, Alexandros Maragakis and Sungjin Im. "The Ethics of Enhanced Interrogations and Torture: A Reappraisal of the Argument." *Ethics & Behavior*, 24.2 (2014): 109–125. http:// www.tandfonline.com/doi/full/10.1080/10508422.2013.814088?scroll=top& needAccess=true

Orwell, George. *1984*. London: Secker & Warburg, 1949.

Pear, Robert. "Investigators Find Repeated Deception in Ads for Drugs." *The New York Times*, 4 December 2002: A22.

Peekhaus, Wilhelm. "A Call to Reclaim Control Over Scholarly Publishing." *Journal of Information Ethics*, 25.2 (Fall 2016): 20–41.

Bibliography

"Peer Review." *Journal of Information Ethics* 7.2 (Fall 1998): entire issue.

Pen America. *And Campus for All: Diversity, Inclusion, and Freedom of Speech at U.S. Universities,* 17 October 2016. New York: Pen America, 2016. https://pen.org/sites/default/files/PEN_campus_report_final_online_2.pdf

Peters, Douglas P., and Stephen J. Ceci. "Peer Review Practices of Psychological Journals: The Fate of Published Articles, Submitted Again" [originally published in] *Behavioral and Brain Sciences,* 5.2 (June 1982): 187–195.

Philipp, Joshua. "Using News as a Weapon." *Epoch Times,* 20–26 May 2016: W1, W4.

"Plagiarism, Part I" and "Plagiarism, Part II." *Journal of Information Ethics,* 3.1 (Spring 1994) and 3.2 (Fall 1994): entire issues.

Pooley, Jefferson. "Metrics Mania: The case against Academia.edu." *The Chronicle of Higher Education,* 12 January 2018: B4–B5.

Poppy, Carrie. "Survey Shows Americans Fear Ghosts, the Government, and Each Other." *Skeptical Inquirer,* 41.1 (January/February 2017): 16–18.

Postman, Neil. *Amusing Ourselves to Death: Public Discourse in the Age of Show Business.* New York: Penguin Books, 1985.

Price, Alan R. "Federal Actions Against Plagiarism in Research." *Journal of Information Ethics,* 5.1 (Spring 1996): 34–51.

"Privacy and Confidentiality." CIRE Current Issues in Research Ethics. http://ccnmtl.columbia.edu/projects/cire/pac/index.html

"The Problem with Higher Education Is_____." *The Chronicle of Higher Education,* 11 November 2016: Section B.

"Publishing Ethics." *Journal of Information Ethics,* 6.1 (Spring 1997): entire issue.

"The Question of Recovery: Slavery, Freedom, and the Archive." *Social Text* 125, 33.4 December 2015): entire issue.

Reich, Eugenie Samuel. *Plastic Fantastic: How the Biggest Fraud in Physics Shook the Scientific World.* New York: Palgrave Macmillan, 2009.

"Research Misconduct." *Journal of Information Ethics,* 5.1 (Spring 1996): entire issue.

Robillard, Kevin. "Ten Journos Caught Fabricating." *Politico* 31 July 2012. http://www.politico.com/story/2012/07/10-journos-caught-fabricating-079221

Robin, Ron. *Scandals and Scoundrels: Seven Cases that Shook the Academy.* Berkeley: University of California Press, 2004.

Rockenbach, Barbara. "Image Ethics: Security and Manipulation of Digital Images." *Journal of Information Ethics,* 9.2 (Fall 2000): 66–71.

Rogers, W. G. *Wise Men Fish Here: The Story of Frances Steloff and the Gotham Book Mart.* New York: Harcourt, Brace & World, 1965.

Ruark, Jennifer. "Anatomy of a Hoax." *The Chronicle of Higher Education,* 6 January 2017: B6–B10.

Ruth, Jeffrey Alfred. *Papers for Pay: Confessions of an Academic Forger.* Jefferson, NC: McFarland, 2015.

Sarokin, David, and Jay Schulkin. *Missed Information: Better Information for a Wealthier, Fairer, and More Sustainable World.* Cambridge, MA: MIT Press, 2016.

Bibliography

Scheutz, Matthias. "The Inherent Dangers of Unidirectional Emotional Bonds between Humans and Social Robots." In *Robot Ethics: The Ethical and Social Implications of Robotics,* edited by Patrick Lin, Keith Abney, and George A. Bekey Cambridge, MA: MIT Press, 2012: 205–221.

Schuessler, Jennifer. "Someone Mailed Feces to Four Philosophers: A Disquisition." *The New York Times,* 8 October 2016: C1–C2.

Science and Engineering Ethics, 1995–.

Scott, Mark. "Europe Presses U.S. Tech Giants to Curb Online Hate Speech." *The New York Times,* 7 December 2016: B4.

———. "Researchers Uncover a Flaw in Europe's Tough Online Privacy Rules." *The New York Times,* 6 June 2016: B3.

Senior, Jennifer. "What Followers You Have, Granny. The Better to Sell to You With, My Dear." Review of *The Attention Merchants* by Tim Wu. *The New York Times,* 3 November 2016: C4.

Severson, Richard J. *The Principles of Information Ethics.* New York: M. E. Sharpe, 1997.

Shane, Scott. "Case of Former N. S. A. Contractor Escalates as Espionage Act Charges Loom." *The New York Times,* 21 October 2016: A12.

Shannon, Claude, and Warren Weaver. *The Mathematical Theory of Communication.* Urbana: University of Illinois Press, 1949.

Shatz, David. *Peer Review: A Critical Inquiry.* Lanham, MD: Rowman & Littlefield, 2004.

Shenk, David. *Data Smog: Surviving the Information Glut.* New York: HarperCollins, 1997.

Shirky, Clay. "People and Technology." Review of *Weapons of Math Destruction: How Big Data Increases Inequality and Threatens Democracy* by Cathy O'Neil. *The New York Times Book Review,* 9 October 2016: 34.

Shweder, Richard A., and Richard E. Nisbett. "Long Sought Research Deregulation Is Upon Us. Don't Squander the Moment." *The Chronicle of Higher Education,* 17 March 2017. A44.

Siegal, Nina. "10 Million Dollar Scandal Shakes the Art World." *The New York Times,* 27 October 2016: C1, C4.

Sisario, Ben, Hawes Spencer, and Sydney Ember. "Magazine Loses Suit Charging Defamation." *The New York Times,* 5 November 2016: B1, B6.

Smith, Martha. "Information Ethics." Ed., Frederick C. Lynden. *Advances in Librarianship* 25. San Diego, CA: Academic Press, 2001: 29–66.

Smith, Martha Montague. "Information Ethics." *Annual Review of Information Science and Technology* 32. Medford, NJ: Information Today, 1997; pp. 339–366.

Smith, Richard. *The Trouble with Medical Journals.* London: Royal Society of Medicine Press, 2006.

Sokal, Alan. "Transgressing the Boundaries: Towards a Transformative Hermeneutics of Quantum Gravity." *Social Text* 46/47, Spring/Summer 1996: 217–252.

Spinello, Richard A. *Cyberethics: Morality and Law in Cyberspace.* 5th ed. Burlington, MA: Jones and Bartlett Learning, 2014.

Bibliography

Stack, Liam. "To Lure Moviegoers, 20th Century Fox Dangles Fake News." *The New York Times*, 16 February 2017: B1, B4.

Stapel, Diederik. *Faking Science: A True Story of Academic Fraud.* Trans. Nicholas J. L. Brown. np: np, 2014. http://nick.brown.free.fr/stapel/FakingScience-20141 214.pdf

Steneck, Nicholas H. *ORI Introduction to the Responsible Conduct of Research.* [Rockville, MD]: Office of Research Integrity, 2007. http://ori.hhs.gov/sites/de fault/files/rcrintro.pdf

Sturges, Paul. "Information Ethics in the Twenty First Century." *Australian Academic & Research Libraries*, 40.4 (2009): 241–251 (original publication). http://www. ifla.org/files/assets/faife/ publications/sturges/information-ethics.pdf

Sully. [Film]. Dir. Clint Eastwood. New York: FilmNation Entertainment, etc., 2016.

Sully 2016. History vs Hollywood. http://www.historyvshollywood.com/reelfaces/ sully/

Surveillance & Society, 2002–.

Tavani, Herman T. *Ethics and Technology: Ethical Issues in an Age of Information and Communication Technology.* 2nd ed. Hoboken, NJ: John Wiley & Sons, 2007.

Tolley, Kim. "Slavery." *Miseducation: A History of Ignorance-Making in America and Abroad*, edited by A. J. Angulo. Baltimore: Johns Hopkins University Press, 2016; pp. 13–33.

Tyler, Colin. "Jeremy Bentham on Open Government and Privacy." *Journal of Information Ethics*, 26.1 (Spring 2017): 112–129.

Victor, Daniel. "Study Urges Stricter Rules for Photo ID Technology." *The New York Times*, 19 October 2016: A16.

Volkman, Richard. "Why Information Ethics Must Begin with Virtue Ethics." *Metaphilosophy*, 41.3 (April 2010): 380–401.

Wager, Elizabeth, Virginia Barbour, Steven Yentis, Sabine Kleinert on behalf of COPE Council. "Retraction Guidelines." Committee on Publication Ethics September 2009. http://publicationethics.org/files/retraction%20guidelines.pdf

Wallach, Wendell, and Colin Allen. *Moral Machines: Teaching Robots Right from Wrong.* New York: Oxford University Press, 2009.

Waller, Bruce N. *Against Moral Responsibility.* Cambridge, MA: MIT Press, 2011.

Warren, Samuel D., and Louis D. Brandeis. "The Right to Privacy." *Harvard Law Review*, IV. 5 (15 December 1890): 193–220.

Weber, Max. *The Protestant Ethic and the Spirit of Capitalism.* New York: Scribner's, 1958.

Weiser, Benjamin. "Hacker Who Broke Into Celebrities' Email Accounts Gets 5 Years in Prison." *The New York Times*, 7 December 2016: A24.

Weller, Ann C. *Editorial Peer Review: Its Strengths and Weaknesses.* Medford, NJ: Information Today, 2001.

Wells, Frank, and Michael Farthing, eds. *Fraud and Misconduct in Biomedical Research.* 4th ed. London: The Royal Society of Medicine Press, 2008.

Wertham, Fredric. *Seduction of the Innocent.* New York: Rinehart, 1954.

Bibliography

Wiener, Norbert. *Cybernetics: Or Control and Communication in the Animal and the Machine.* New York: Wiley, 1948.

Witkowski, Tomasz, and Maciej Zatonski. *Psychology Gone Wrong: The Dark Sides of Science and Therapy.* Boca Raton, FL: Brownwalker Press, 2015.

Wu, Tim. "Content Confusion." Review of *Black Ops Advertising* by Mara Einstein. *The New York Times Book Review*, 27 November 2016: 21.

Zimbardo, Phillip. *"The Lucifer Effect: Understanding How Good People Turn Evil."* New York: Random House, 2007.

Index

Index

Index

insurance 141
imaging 163–166; evidence 165–166; manipulation 165
Imanishi-Kari, Thereza 60
Index Librorum Prohibitorum 90
information 17ff; classes of 19; history 17–18; quantum 18; storage 10
informational justice 121
institutional review boards 53
intellectual freedom 88–95; college 127
Internet 53, 89, 112; ethics 100–105; fraud 140; sexual material 103; of things 114; trolling 102
Internet Archive 125
Internet research ethics 53, 54
Ioannidis, John 52
IRIE 5, 6, 47
Israel, Lee 70–71

Jackson, Ben 120
Jacoby, Susan 29
Jenkins, Holman W., Jr. 115
Johnson, Deborah 52, 97, 98, 99
Jones, Meg Leta 124, 125
Journal of Technoethics: topics 13–14
JT LeRoy 71
Jung, Carl 66
The Jungle 91, 142

Kahane, Jack 92
Kakutani, Michiko 29
Kant, Immanuel 32
Kennedy, John F. 159
Kinko 122
Klein, Marty 103
Knowles, Alonzo 97
Kosinsky, Jerzy 75
the Kronhausens 103
Kuhn, Thomas 58
Kujau, Konrad 70

LaFollette, Marcel 60
law 38ff, 117ff; national differences 118
Lawrence Livermore National Laboratory 129
Lee, Vu 16
Leiter, Brian 131
Lessig, Lawrence 101
librarians disallowed to speak 119

Lindner, Robert 148
Lingua Franca 68
Lipinski, Tomas 121
Lipstadt, Deborah 27
literature: forgeries, fraud 70–71
lobbying 118

Machlup, Fritz 19
MacKinnon, Catherine 92, 93, 94, 97
MacNeil, Heather 86
Macpherson, James 70
Madoff, Bernard 38
The Making of a Woman Surgeon 146
Mallon, Thomas 71
Manning, Bradley (now Chelsea) 39, 111, 120
Maret, Susan 89
Marlatt, Greta E. 162
Martin, Brian 22
Marx, Gary 106, 113, 116
Marx, Johannes 159
Mathiesen, Kay 49
McClintock, Barbara 59
Mead, Margaret 64
medicine 144–149; confidentiality 147–148; education 145–146; information 148–149; misinformation 146–147
Menand, Louis 92
Milgram, Stanley 57
Mill, John Stuart 32
Mindless 136
misinformation 20ff
misplaced belief 22–24
Mitchell, William J. 166
Mitnick, Kevin 97
Mitroff, Ian 58
Monahan, Torin 115
Monmonier, Mark 25
Moran, Gordon 91
Morgan, Elizabeth 146
Morozov, Evgeny 89
Morris, Robert T, Jr. 97
music: quotation 71

Nabokov, Vladimir 118
Nader, Ralph 135
NASA 86
National Coalition Against Censorship 95

Index

Index